Beechcraft Pursuit of Perfection

A History of Beechcraft Airplanes

Edward H. Phillips

FLYING BOOKS

1401 Kings Wood Rd.
Eagan, Minnesota 55122

For more than 60 years, the Beech Aircraft Corporation has been recognized worldwide as a premier builder of high quality, high performance business and personal airplanes.

In BEECHCRAFT – PURSUIT OF PERFECTION, every airplane the company has built commercially is presented along with a description containing pertinent data and highlights. Experimental and limited-production designs also are included and represent some of the most interesting Beechcrafts to leave the drawing boards and take to the skies.

To supplement photographs and to provide additional technical information, three-view drawings have been included throughout the book for the benefit of the Beechcraft aficionado as well as researchers and history buffs.

In addition, three appendices in the back of the book provide data on Approved Type Certificates, constructor (serial) number listings by year and model and footnotes pertaining to specific Beechcraft airplanes.

The author expresses his sincere thanks to Beech Aircraft Corporation and Raytheon Company officials for their assistance in making historical, production and archival material available.

Special thanks to Dora Thomas, Mary Hall, Gib Urick, Bob Umscheid, Don St. Peter, Bob Magness, Jan Gustafson, Roger Hubble, Dick Mullen, Lyn Roberts, Cecil Bundy, Jim Lary, Phyllis McCabe, Jo Will, Annie Johnson, Lloyd Aldrich, Barbara Harding, Max Prickett, John Cook, Jim Zluticky and Kenny Freeman of the Beechcraft Photo Lab, and especially to Mike Potts and Pat Zerbe of Beech Aircraft Corporation's Public Relations office.

Additional thanks to Eric Griffin, Lou Johansen, Bud Francis and other pilots in the company's Engineering Flight Test office for providing information on first flights and experimental aircraft data.

Credit:
Cover Photo: Beechjet 400A over Wichita. Photograph by Paul Bowen.

Other Aviation Titles from Flying Books

Wings of Cessna, Model 120 to the Citation III
by Edward H. Phillips

Cessna, A Master's Expression
by Edward H. Phillips

Travel Air, Wings Over the Prairie
by Edward H. Phillips

Piper Airplanes – A Legacy Aloft
by Edward H. Phillips

Speed, the Biography of Charles Holman
by Noel Allard

The 91 Before Lindbergh
by Peter Allen

DH-88: The Story of DeHavilland's Racing Comets
by David Ogilvy

Of Monocoupes and Men
by John Underwood

The Stinsons
by John Underwood

Aircraft Service Manual Reprints
Piper J-3 Cub
Aeronca 7AC Champ
Aeronca 11AC Chief
Taylorcraft BC-12D

Walter H. Beech

Olive Ann Beech

Walter and Olive Ann Beech were a team, a talented couple who had but one goal: to manufacture the finest airplanes in the world. Their enthusiasm, drive and determination to succeed was founded on far more than just building flying machines; it was built upon the solid rock of quality, strengthened by integrity in business and piloted by the unshakeable belief that a satisfied customer was the company's most important asset.

These values were an integral part of the organization from its genesis in April 1932 through economic depression, the horrors of global war and the blessings of peace. At the company's helm until his death in 1950, Walter Herschel Beech became one of America's most respected and honored aeronautical entrepreneurs and an aviation legend in his own time.

But Mr. Beech was only half the team. At his side was Olive Ann Beech, who shared equally in her husband's desire to establish an aircraft company on the Plains of her native Kansas. In addition to having acknowledged talent for financial matters, Mrs. Beech possessed the ability to apply her acumen to the essential, daily affairs of the airplane business.

Upon Walter Beech's death, Olive Ann Beech assumed the duties of company leadership and met challenge after challenge without fail. Like her husband, she wasn't afraid to push Beech Aircraft Corporation onward and upward, encouraging innovation and application of advanced technology to new airplanes that set the pace for competitors to follow.

Yet, leadership alone does not ensure a company's success. The unfailing efforts of Beech employees, from vice presidents to production line workers, have contributed their skills and abilities to make Beechcraft airplanes the best that money can buy.

"BEECHCRAFT – PURSUIT OF PERFECTION" is respectfully dedicated to Walter H. Beech, Olive Ann Beech and every Beechcrafter since 1932. Together they founded a kingdom whose realm is not of the earth but of the sky. ℞

Copyright © 1992 Flying Books, Publishers and Wholesalers, 1401 Kings Wood Road, Eagan, Minnesota 55122

First edition 1987, Flying Books, Title: Beechcraft – Staggerwing to Starship

Library of Congress Cataloging in Publication Data   Phillips, Edward H.
Beechcraft
Pursuit of Perfection,
A History of Beechcraft Airplanes

ISBN 0-911139-11-7

Printed in the United States of America.

On November 5, 1932 pilot William "Pete" Hill took the first Beechcraft Model 17R aloft, thundering into the chilly Kansas air behind a 420 hp Wright radial engine. Lifted into the blue skies on its negative-stagger wings, the biplane's flight marked the successful debut of a classic airplane and a humble start for the infant Beech Aircraft Company.

Walter and Olive Ann Beech, together with engineer Theodore A. "Ted" Wells and business associate K.K. Shaul, had formed the company in April 1932. Aviation was not new to the foursome—all of them had worked together at the Wichita, Kansas-based Travel Air Co. in the late 1920s.

Mr. Beech had served as president and a secretary named Olive Ann Mellor kept the office running smoothly. Wells was a young, aeronautical engineering graduate who came to Travel Air in 1928, and Shaul had been comptroller of the firm.

Sold to the giant Curtiss-Wright Corporation in the summer of 1929, Travel Air continued to flourish as one of America's foremost airplane manufacturers until the Great Depression clipped its wings in 1931.

During his tenure with Travel Air, Walter Beech learned the complex workings of the airplane business. He became a nationally-known aviator and was recognized throughout the budding light aircraft industry as a pragmatic businessman and expert salesman.

Olive Ann Mellor, who had distinguished herself as Travel Air's office manager, married Walter Beech in 1930. She possessed a keen understanding and appreciation for the financial workings of the company and had learned much about flying machines, aviators and how the industry functioned.

Despite Mr. Beech's position as a vice president with Curtiss-Wright, he was a restless man who tolerated flying a desk in New York City but yearned to build airplanes in Kansas.

In the spring of 1932, Walter and Olive Ann Beech decided to risk all they had to get back into the airplane business. Armed with courage, self-confidence, determination and their life savings, the couple and their trusted associates returned to Wichita—a city known as the "Air Capital of the World."

Although Mr. Beech had planned to locate the new company in the abandoned Travel Air facilities on East Central Avenue, the factory Beech had helped to build was not available. Room was found, however, in the empty Cessna Aircraft Co. factory on Franklin Road southeast of the city.

In an interesting twist of fate, the Beech Aircraft Co. began building Ted Wells' biplane in Clyde Cessna's monoplane factory. Following the first flight, Wells and his tiny staff that included Cessna's nephew Dwane L. Wallace, refined the 17R and began work on a smaller, less powerful version featuring retractable landing gear.

Sales were slow during the company's first two years of existence, but by 1934 the Beechcraft Model 17 started to sell in larger numbers. With profits in hand, Mr. Beech leased the Travel Air factory in April, 1934, to accommodate increasing demand for Beechcraft biplanes.

To Walter and Olive Ann Beech, returning to the hallowed halls of Travel Air was like coming home—a home that would grow to eventually become world headquarters for the company. They purchased the entire five-building complex for $150,000 from Curtiss-Wright in January 1937.

By 1934, the days of the large and powerful Model 17R series were coming to an end. The last of the leviathan biplanes was the A17F powered by a 690 hp Wright radial powerplant. Big and fast, the airplane had a maximum speed of nearly 250 mph—faster than aircraft flown by the U.S. Army Air Corps or the U.S. Navy at that time.

To stay in business, however, Walter Beech knew the big biplanes had to be superceded in production by smaller, more affordable aircraft designed to sell in a Depression market.

In 1934, the company introduced the Model B17L powered by a 225 hp Jacobs radial engine. With retractable gear and economical operating costs, the B17L sold well but was replaced in 1936 by the C17 series. The C17B was powered by a 285 hp Jacobs engine, the C17L used a 225 hp Jacobs and the C17R featured a 420 hp Wright radial powerplant.

Wells and his small engineering staff continued to refine the biplanes and in 1937 introduced the D17 series that represented an entirely new generation of the now famous Model 17 Beechcraft biplane.

The aircraft boasted improved ailerons, full-width lower wing flaps, a redesigned empennage and higher gross weights. Three versions were offered: the D17A with 350 hp Wright engine; D17R with a 420 hp Wright radial and the D17S with 450 hp Pratt & Whitney Wasp powerplant that became the most prolific version of any Model 17 produced.

Although biplanes still reigned supreme on the production line in 1935, a new Beechraft was needed to expand the

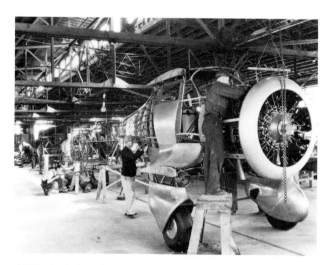

A17F c/n 5, NC12583, is shown here under construction in the former Cessna Aircraft Co. facilities leased by Walter Beech from 1932 to 1934. Note Cessna DC-6A and DC-6B monoplane fuselages stored overhead.

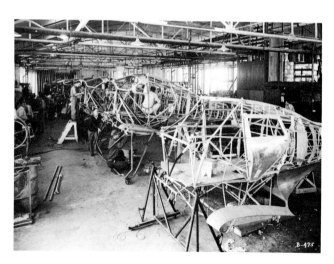

Model 17 biplanes were meticulously manufactured by hand. Each Staggerwing was essentially a custom-built airplane. (Jim Horne collection).

company's product line. Mr. Beech put Ted Wells and his engineers to work designing the Model 18 monoplane equipped with two engines, all-metal construction and a cabin for six occupants.

Designed for flying executives and the charter airlines, the Model 18 first flew in January 1937. The aircraft quickly established itself as a rugged light transport, particularly in Canada where Model 18s operated on wheels, floats and skis with equal reliability.

The Beech Aircraft Company reached a major milestone in 1939 by posting its first million-dollar sales year. The Model D17 biplanes were selling well, and the Model 18 monoplanes were becoming increasingly popular with customers around the world.

As World War II broke out in Europe, the company's export business was accounting for a significant amount of total sales compared with previous years. The company's airplanes were being flown in 23 countries around the globe—testimony to the high level of quality and dependability built into every Beechcraft.

By 1940 the clouds of war had enveloped virtually all of Europe and threatened to end America's self-imposed isolationism. Walter and Olive Ann Beech knew that if the United States went to war, their company would be called upon to produce aircraft for the cause of freedom.

Anticipating much higher demand, Mr. Beech stretched the company's financial power to the limit and secured money from the government's Reconstruction Finance Company to rapidly expand production facilities.

The engineering department began working hard and long hours to design versions of the Model 18 suitable for training the thousands of fledgling pilots, navigators and bombardiers.

Before the Imperial Japanese Navy attacked Pearl Harbor on December 7, 1941 Beech was already producing the AT-11 bombing trainer for the U.S. Army and the SNB gunnery trainer for the U.S. Navy. Further developments led to the AT-7 and SNB-2 navigation trainers and the C-45 military transport used widely for liaison and general cargo duties.

Early in the war, Beech engineers led by Ted Wells created the twin-engine AT-10, known officially as the Model 25 initially and then as the Model 26. Built primarily of plywood to conserve aluminum, the AT-10 helped train military pilots to fly complex, multi-engine aircraft such as the Boeing B-17 and Consolidated B-24 heavy bombers.

Although the AT-11, AT-10 and SNB series dominated wartime contracts, the D17S was not overlooked for duty. Designated as the UC-43 for the U.S. Army and the GB-1 and GB-2 for the U.S. Navy, the rough-and-ready biplanes served with distinction in the European, Pacific and China-Burma-India Theaters of War as fast personnel and light cargo transports, and performed lead navigation flights for island-hopping fighters and bombers in the Pacific.

In 1943, the Douglas Aircraft Company called upon Beech

Beech Aircraft Company factory, located in ex-Travel Air buildings, on East Central Avenue, Wichita, Kansas in 1934, soon after Beech leased the facility from Curtiss-Wright and transferred production from Cessna factory.

to produce wing and nacelle assemblies for the A-26 "Invader" medium bomber being produced by Douglas in Tulsa, Oklahoma. Beechcrafters from the president himself down to the newest employee and a myriad of subcontractors swiftly responded to the call. When production ceased in 1945, Beech had built 1,635 complete sets and delivered them to Douglas on or ahead of schedule.

As the Allied war effort gained momentum in 1944, the U.S. Army Air Force's need for a ground attack aircraft with heavy firepower was met with the XA-38 "Grizzly," designated as the Model 28 "Destroyer" by the company. Only two aircraft were built and both performed admirably during extensive flight and armament testing, but by 1945 the war was drawing to a close and the need for an advanced ground attack aircraft was deemed unnecesary.

In 1945, victory in Europe and the defeat of Japan meant that Beechcrafters could at last lay down their swords. In 1932, the company had fewer than 10 employees. By 1937, 220 workers were building Beechcrafts. In the spring of 1940, employment reached 780 and then soared to 2,354 people in April 1941 before the ranks swelled to 10,950 in 1943 and peaked at 14,110 in February 1945.

Over a six-year period, hard-working, dedicated Beechcrafters had built nearly 7,400 airplanes. In recognition of this effort, the company was awarded the prestigious Army/Navy E award for efficiency five times during the war—a tribute to Beech Aircraft Corporation's reputation for consistently

Inflight view of first Model 18 with 320 hp Wright powerplants.

AT-11 formation over the desert Southwest on a training flight.

Profile view of powerful XA-38 Grizzly. Note wing hardpoint, entry ladder below center fuselage section.

producing the weapons of war.

The company began making the transition from wartime to peacetime production in late 1944, when Beechcraft engineers began designing the D18S version of the veteran Model 18. Improvements included a gross weight 20% higher than that of the pre-war Model 18S with Pratt & Whitney R-985 radial engines, redesigned landing gear, longer nacelles and a new instrument panel.

When introduced in the summer of 1945, the D18S held the distinction of being the first commercial, multi-engine airplane seating up to nine occupants to receive an Approved Type Certificate after the war.

The new Beechcraft sold well, and production quickly reached two per day as companies denied wartime aircraft purchases rushed to place their orders. Beech also introduced the Model 18C/18CT—a special version designed specifically for service with small, commuter airlines.

Walter H. Beech knew the future lay with the all-metal monoplane, not fabric-covered biplanes. Yet, he believed there was a market for the aging but superlative Model 17. Changes were made to the D17S to create the G17S—the final variant of Theodore Well's classic biplane.

A new, longer engine cowling surrounded the Pratt & Whitney Wasp radial engine, and along with a larger empennage and redesigned instrument panel, were the essential elements that completed the transformation.

The cost of manufacturing the G17S, however, was simply too high. Most of the airplane was hand-made, especially the wood wings and complex fairings. Many of the parts and assemblies were unsuitable to modern, mass production techniques embraced by Beech.

Although Mr. Beech knew the G17S was the best Model 17 built, the fact that it cost too much to build meant that it would cost too much to buy. Priced at $29,000 with a new engine, the venerable biplane was economically unacceptable to produce. Only 20 were built.

By comparison, the new, all-metal Model 35 Bonanza that entered production in 1946 was priced at a mere $7,975, carried four people in comfort and flew at 180 mph.

Initial deliveries of the Bonanza began in February 1947. One Bonanza became the most famous Beechcraft when Captain William P. Odom flew the fourth Model 35 built—named the "Waikiki Beech"—5,273 miles nonstop from Honolulu, Territory of Hawaii to Teterboro Airport, Teterboro, New Jersey in March 1949.

In an attempt to meet growing postwar demand for a small, economical commuter airliner, Beech Aircraft Corporation introduced the Model 34 Twin Quad in 1947. Like its famous Bonanza sibling, the Twin Quad featured a V-tail but carried up to 20 passengers.

The high wing monoplane's unique powerplant installation consisted of two piston engines coupled together driving a single propeller through a common gearbox. Although the Model 34 was a promising design, the small airliner market failed to materialize and the project was terminated in 1949. Only one airplane was built.

As the 1950s arrived, the company lost one of its founders and its president when Walter H. Beech died on November 29, 1950. Olive Ann Beech succeeded her husband as president and chief executive officer of the company in December. In keeping with the Beechcraft tradition, business contin-

August 2, 1948 photograph of Model 34 Twin Quad.

U.S. Air Force T-34A on acceptance flight over Kansas Plains.

ued, although Mr. Beech's aeronautical expertise and entrepreneurial spirit would be sorely missed.

In the previous year before Mr. Beech's death, the company had introduced the Model 45 Mentor, a two-seat military trainer derived from the Model 35 Bonanza. In 1950, the U.S. Air Force ordered a YT-34, followed by a production order for an initial batch of T-34s to train cadet pilots.

The Mentor's popularity soon spread to the U.S. Navy, which ordered the T-34B version in 1953. Based at Cory Field, Pensacola, Florida, the T-34B served the Navy as its primary trainer until the late 1970s, when the advanced, turboprop Beechcraft T-34C replaced the aging Mentors.

In export configuration, the Model 45 garnered a $1 million order from Chile in 1953. Other Central and South American countries including Argentina, Colombia, El Salvador and Venezuela received aircraft to train their pilots. Mexico, Spain and Turkey also bought trainers.

In 1953, Japan's Fuji Heavy Industries, Inc., was granted a license by Beech Aircraft Corporation to build the Model 45, followed by the Canadian Car and Foundry Co., Ltd., that produced a version for the Royal Canadian Air Force. Argentina also built Mentors under license, the aircraft being assembled from kits built at the Wichita factory.

The Model 50 Twin Bonanza and the abortive T-36A twin-engine military trainer were two new Beechcrafts introduced in 1949 and 1951 respectively. Designed to meet a U.S. Air Force requirement for a fast, pressurized pilot trainer, the sole T-36A built never flew.

On the morning of its scheduled first flight, the Air Force cancelled the contract and the prototype T-36A was scrapped. The Model 50, however, went on to become a popular airplane with businessmen and pilots alike.

During the Korean War, Beechcrafters built jettisonable fuel and napalm tanks for the military as well as complete wing assemblies for the Lockheed T-33 jet and ailerons for Boeing's innovative B-47 "Stratojet" bomber.

Despite the war effort, commercial sales remained strong in the early 1950s, and Beech engineers continued to develop new aircraft for the burgeoning general aviation market. The Model 73 Jet Mentor was developed in response to a U.S. Navy and U.S. Air Force requirement for an advanced, jet-powered trainer. Based largely on the piston-powered T-34, the Model 73 prototype first flew in December 1955, but did not receive a production order from either service.

The first flight of another new Beechcraft occurred in August 1956, when the Model 95 Travel Air roared aloft. Offered as a lightweight twin-engine airplane, the Travel Air bridged the gap between the single-engine Bonanza and the larger Twin Bonanza.

By 1958, the ubiquitous Model 18 had evolved into the Super 18 and maintained a firm grip on its share of the heavy piston-twin market. That year, the company also introduced the improved F50 and D50 Twin Bonanzas and the J35 Bonanza, with its fuel-injected engine.

In July, a J35 Beechcraft Bonanza made aviation history when pilot Marion "Pat" Boling flew the "Philippine Bonanza" from the Manila International Airport near Luzon, Philippines, to Pendelton, Oregon, in 45 hours, 43 minutes. The odyssey broke the non-stop record held by William Odom since 1949. Boling's triumphant flight once again echoed the adage that "It takes a Beechcraft to beat a Beechcraft!"

The Model Super 18 series was joined on the production lines by the Model 65 Queen Air in 1959. The Queen Air, and the U.S. Army L-23F version that preceded it, both evolved from the Twin Bonanza. Beechcraft engineers enlarged the cabin and mounted two Lycoming 340 hp geared, piston engines.

In addition to expanding its twin-engine product line, the

Experimental Model 35 Bonanza in flight. A classic design.

company also introduced the Model 33 Debonair in 1959, providing buyers with a less expensive, straight-tail version of the Model 35 Bonanza without sacrificing performance.

The Debonair was followed in 1961 by the introduction of the Model 55 Baron series. Capable of carrying up to five occupants, the Baron had a maximum speed of 236 mph. and paved the way for future versions such as the Model 58, turbocharged 58TC and pressurized 58P that were developed in the 1970s.

To expand its light, single-engine product line, in 1963 Beech Aircraft Corporation introduced the four-place Model 23 "Musketeer," aimed at the entry-level segment of the market. Although initial production aircraft were built in Wichita, production was shifted in 1964 to Liberal, Kansas, where all subsequent Musketeer derivatives, including the Sundowner and Sierra, were built.

The company's enormous success with the Super 18 series and the later Queen Air gave impetus to what would become one of Beech Aircraft Corporation's crowning achievements: development of the turboprop-powered Model 90 King Air.

Using Pratt & Whitney PT6A-6 engines, the Model 90 truly heralded a new era in the Beechcraft dynasty—the turbine era that would make King Airs the world's most popular corporate turboprop aircraft and propel the company to new heights of success.

The King Air evolved from the Model 87—a Queen Air airframe modified with PT6 turboprop engines that had been undergoing flight tests since May 1963. Pressurized and fast with a maximum speed of 280 mph., the Model 90 quickly established itself as the flagship of the Beechcraft fleet.

The demand for higher performance in the piston-twin market led to development of the pressurized Model 60 Duke, which made its first flight in December 1966. With

Prototype Model 50 Twin-Bonanza ready for maiden flight, November, 1949. Test pilot was Vern L. Carstens.

Flight view of Pat Boling's record-setting "Philippine Bonanza", N35U. Note wing tip tanks.

1960 Model G18S at the Beech factory. Note two-piece windshield, aerodynamic wing tips and taller tailwheel structure.

rakish styling and cabin accomodations for six occupants, the Duke fit between the Baron and the larger King Air.

Frank E. Hedrick, who had served as the company's executive vice president since 1960, became the third president of Beech Aircraft Corporation in January 1968. Mrs. Olive Ann Beech continued to serve as chairman of the board and chief executive officer.

The Model 99, a turboprop 17-seat commuter airliner, made its debut in 1968 as did the six-seat Model 36 Bonanza. With a maximum speed of 204 mph and a range of nearly 1,000 statute miles, the new Bonanza featured double doors on the right fuselage side to ease loading and unloading of passengers and cargo. The Model A36 would prove to be the most versatile and popular of all Bonanzas in the years ahead.

In 1969, the Model 100 King Air took to the skies above Wichita. With a longer fuselage and more room in the cabin, it superceded the Model 90 King Air as the company's premier product.

After building more than 7,000 airplanes—in at least 32 different configurations of commercial and military derivatives—the company terminated production of the Model 18 in November 1969. The last three airplanes, all Super H18 versions, were delivered to Japan Air Lines, ending 32 years of continuous production.

The six-seat Model 58 Baron was introduced in the 1970 model year and featured the same double doors found on the Model A36 Bonanza. The Baron 58 quickly became one of the best selling twin-engine airplanes in the Beechcraft kingdom, primarily because of the airplane's useful load, high speed and ability to operate from rough, unimproved fields.

With the advent of the space age in the 1950s, Beech Aircraft Corporation became deeply involved with the United

State's space program. Early developmental work began in 1954 when the company performed secret research into the use of cryogenics as possible sources of oxygen for breathing and for electrical power aboard future U.S. space vehicles. By 1962, the company's Aerospace Division located at Boulder, Colorado, had succeeded in designing a practical system for loading cryogenic materials on the National Aeronautics and Space Administration's Gemini spacecraft.

The liquid oxygen was critical to the survival of the two Gemini astronauts because they depended on the Beechcraft system to supply both capsule pressurization and oxygen for breathing. Later, company engineers designed ground support equipment for NASA's lunar excursion module for the Apollo program that put Americans on the moon in July 1969.

Another key part of the company's expanding technology base was its Missile Division that was busy throughout the 1960s developing advanced target drones such as the Mach 2 KD2B-1, that entered service in 1961 with the U.S. Air Force and U.S. Navy. Another target, the Model 1025, was used extensively by the military for training anti-aircraft weapons crews.

The division also developed the MQM-107B subsonic target designed to help train crews manning ground-based, air defense weapons systems. Capable of simulating multiple targets, the MQM-107B proved to be a valuable training asset for the U.S. Army.

To train U.S. Navy aviators and sailors against airborne supersonic threats, Beech's missile division designed the Mach 3.0 AQM-37C target. Air-launched, the missile was capable of flying attack profiles at low, medium or high altitudes.

With the dawning of the 1970s, Beech Aircraft Corporation continued to develop the highly successful King Air se-

Model F90 prototype c/n LA-1 became engineering testbed c/n LE-0 in 1980. Garrett AiResearch TPE-331 engines were installed for testing as possible Model G90 that never evolved. Beech also tested more streamlined, raked windshield design on LE-0.

Illustration of Beech T-36A for USAF. Only one was built and never flew. Project was cancelled morning of test flight in 1953.

ries. The company delivered its 1,000th turboprop-powered airplane in 1972—less than 10 years after the Model 90's first flight.

Never content to rest on their laurels, Beechcraft engineers unleashed the Model 200 Super King Air in 1973, culminating a four-year development program. The Model 200 became Beechcraft's latest flagship, with 850 shp. Pratt & Whitney Canada PT6A-41 turboprop engines, a graceful, T-tail empennage and increased cabin room for eight passengers and two pilots.

Touted by Beech officials as the most thoroughly tested Beechcraft airplane built to date, the Super King Air set a new standard for turboprop corporate aircraft and embarked on a career that has made it a legend in its own time.

The year of 1972 was also the 25th anniversary of the Beechcraft Model 35 Bonanza. To celebrate the occasion, a specially-painted V35B Bonanza toured the nation, appropriately registered as N25AB. More than 10,000 Model 35s would be produced before production ceased in 1982.

In 1973, NASA's Skylab orbiting observatory used Beechcraft-designed cryogenic systems to provide life support for the astronauts, and in 1974, the company was selected to supply the power reactant storage assembly for the space shuttle orbiter program. The system supplied liquid oxygen for the shuttle's life support systems, and liquid oxygen and liquid hydrogen to produce on-board electrical power. A by-product was drinking water.

On a more down-to-Earth scale, the company's engineers further improved the Model 58 Baron series by developing the pressurized 58P that was introduced in 1974. Two years later in 1976, the Model B100 King Air made its debut. Powered by two Garrett TPE-331 turboprop engines, the B100 offered an alternative powerplant to the Pratt & Whitney Canada PT6A series that powered the Model 90, A100 and Model 200 King Airs.

Twelve years after introducing the trend-setting Model 90 in 1964, the company had expanded its family of King Airs to five models: the C90, E90, A100, B100 and Model 200 Super King Air. More than 1,300 of the aircraft had been sold, testifying to the King Air's established popularity as the world's foremost turboprop business aircraft.

As it had done with its top-of-the-line King Airs, Beech Aircraft Corporation also expanded its commitment to the entry-level, light aircraft market in the late 1970s by introducing two new airplanes—the Model 76 Duchess lightweight twin-engine trainer in 1978 and the single-engine Model 77 Skipper in 1979.

Both aircraft were developed to equip Beechcraft Aero Clubs across the nation with modern, state-of-the-art trainers. The Duchess and Skipper sported T-tails and bonded aluminum honeycomb construction pioneered on the Model 23 Musketeer of 1961.

The company celebrated another historic milestone in February 1977 when the 10,000th Model 35 Bonanza rolled off the Wichita assembly line. The airplane was flown on a nationwide tour to denote the Bonanza's 30-year dominance of the high performance, single-engine market. That same year, the 1,000th Model 36 Bonanza was delivered to its owner.

As the decade of the 1970s drew to a close, continued success of the Super King Air pushed Beechcraft sales to new heights. In 1978, a Model 200 became the 2,000 King Air built, and in 1979 the new F90 King Air was unveiled as the sixth member of the company's growing fleet of corporate turboprops.

Powered by two Pratt & Whitney Canada PT6A-135 engines rated at 750 shp. each, the F90 embodied all the improvements of the earlier Model 90 series, coupled with the T-tail empennage of the Super King Air. It was the first King Air to incorporate the company's advanced, multi-bus electrical system.

In their never-ending quest for more performance, Beechcraft engineers introduced the turbocharged Model A36TC Bonanza in 1979. Boasting 300 hp. and designed to cruise at 25,000 feet, the A36TC marked the company's return to the turbocharged segment of the single-engine market after a nine-year absence.

The A36TC was followed in 1982 by the B36TC that featured a greater wingspan, 102-gallon fuel capacity, a new instrument panel and specially-designed, wingtip-mounted vortex generators derived from NASA technology.

After 48 years of ownership under the Beech name and nearly five decades of unparalleled success, Beech Aircraft Corporation became a wholly-owned subsidiary of the Lexington, Massachusetts-based Raytheon Company on February 8, 1980.

Raytheon's chief product line centers on high technology electronics, including radars and weapons systems, as well as production of commercial appliance products. The company also is active in industry services and publishing.

Its program of diversification, coupled with Beech Aircraft Corporation's desire to ally itself with an organization dedicated to the future of aviation, assured that the merger would be mutually beneficial.

In addition to acquiring a new owner, the company also introduced a new Beechcraft in 1980. The 17-seat Model C99, upgraded from the earlier B99 of 1972, featured Pratt & Whitney Canada PT6A-36 turboprop engines, an improved hydraulic landing gear system and a higher gross weight of 11,300 lb.

Frank E. Hedrick, who came to work for Walter H. Beech in 1940, stepped down as president of Beech Aircraft Corporation in January 1981 to become vice chairman of the board and chairman of the executive committee. Edward C. Burns became the company's fourth president. Mrs. Olive Ann Beech remained chairman of the board.

Like her famous husband, Mrs. Beech had become an aviation legend in her own time. Her exemplary leadership of the world's premier business airplane manufacturer had earned her not only the respect and admiration of many people within the industry, but gave rise to her universal recognition as America's First Lady of Aviation.

In July 1981 Mrs. Beech was honored for her many contributions to aeronautics when she was inducted into the Aviation Hall of Fame at ceremonies held in Dayton, Ohio. Mr. Beech had been inducted posthumously in July 1977.

The Model C-99 embodied key system improvements over earlier models and was a popular choice for small regional airlines in the 1980's.

As the King Air line continued to assert its market dominance into the early 1980s, the Super King Air was upgraded in 1981 to Model B200 configuration by increasing cabin pressurization differential, improving interior comfort and installing Pratt & Whitney Canada PT6A-42 turboprop engines that increased climb performance.

The year 1982 marked not only the 50th anniversary of the company's founding, but also a major transition for Beechcraft management. Mrs. Beech, Frank Hedrick and Edward Burns announced their retirements, creating new leadership opportunities.

Linden S. Blue became president of the company that year, and in 1983 Beech introduced its revolutionary Model 2000 Starship. Christened with a name as advanced as the aircraft itself, the Starship's unique composite construction used graphite carbon epoxy and Nomex honeycomb materials instead of conventional aluminum alloys.

The aircraft's highly advanced electronic flight instrument system avionic suite, designed by Rockwell International's Collins General Aviation Division, consisted of 14 cathode ray tubes to make Starship's flight deck the most advanced cockpit found in any business aircraft.

The Starship project was guided through its initial design stages by Linden Blue before James S. Walsh took the helm of Beech Aircraft Corporation in 1984. Under Walsh's leadership, the company forged ahead with Starship development before Max E. Bleck became the company's seventh president in May 1987.

Bleck led the company through the certification and introduction of the Starship. His broad expertise as an engineer, pilot and business executive were key factors in the success of the program.

As Starship development moved forward, further improvement and evolution of the company's traditional product line continued unabated. The Model 1900 Airliner was announced in 1983 as a 19-seat regional transport featuring a 16,600 lb. maximum gross weight and Pratt & Whitney Canada PT6A-65B turboprop powerplants.

Based largely on the Super King Air B200 airframe, the production 1900 version had a lengthened fuselage to accommodate the additional seats. A multi-bus electrical system and 3,000 psi. hydraulic landing gear system, and a wing with a multi-element, continous wing spar were other major design features. Seventy-four Model 1900s were built before production ended in 1986.

Entering service with regional airlines in late 1983, the 1900 evolved into a mature regional airliner, with increased fuel capacity and improved systems. The Air National Guard received six of the long-range 1900s beginning in 1987, designated C-12J and used primarily for transport missions.

Developed simultaneously with the Model 1900, the Model 300 Super King Air was introduced in 1984. With its 1,050 shp turboprop engines, 14,000 lb. maximum gross weight and four-blade propellers, the Model 300 quickly established itself as the king of all King Airs. Its high rate of climb up to an operating altitude of 35,000 feet was enthusiastically received by corporate operators.

To provide Beechcraft customers with a logical step-up airplane from the Model 300, in 1985 the company acquired the design and production rights for the Japanese Mitsubishi Diamond business jet.

Powered by two Pratt & Whitney Canada JT15-D turbofan engines, the Diamond was renamed the "Beechjet 400" and a new interior, optional thrust reversers and increased fuel capacity transformed the sleek jet into the company's premier business aircraft.

In 1987, the Beechcraft King Air series captured nearly 90 percent of the twin-engine turboprop market, and the venerable A36 and F33A Bonanzas were the best selling, single-engine high performance aircraft for the third consecutive year.

The popular Beechjet 400 had garnered 21 percent of the light jet market in 1988, demonstrating its high sales potential. Based on that success, Beech officials decided to purchase all tooling and fixtures from the Japanese and began shifting manufacturing operations from Mitsubishi's facilities in Nagoya to Beechcraft's Salina and Wichita facilities. The transfer was completed in July 1989.

A program to upgrade the Beechjet 400 culminated in FAA certification of the Beechjet 400A in July 1990, and initial deliveries began at the end of the year. Key improvements included a higher maximum speed of 468 knots, heavier maximum gross weight of 16,100 lb. and an increased certified operating altitude of 45,000 ft. Sixty-three Beechjet 400s had been sold before the 400A replaced it on the production line.

Beechcraft introduced the Model 350 Super King Air in October 1989, and the aircraft rapidly became the most successful new King Air developed by the company. Focusing on increased cabin comfort, Beechcraft engineers lengthened the Model 300's fuselage 34 inches and developed an entirely new interior to complement the additional room for passengers.

The airplane was certified under the stringent rules of Federal Aviation Regulation Part 23 through Amendment 34, and featured composite winglets and a five-tube electronic flight instrument system as standard equipment. An instant sales success, more than 60 Model 350s had been delivered by the end of 1991, and a cargo door version was also available as an option.

1990 was a banner year for Beech Aircraft Corporation. The company achieved its best fiscal year since 1981 by posting total sales of $1.1 billion—marking a significant first-time achievement in its history.

In February, a team of Beech Aircraft Corporation, McDonnell Douglas and Quintron Corporation was selected by the U.S. Air Force to provide aircraft, training and flight simulators respectively for the service's next-generation Tanker Transport Training System.

Beechcraft's contribution to the winning effort centered on development of a military version of the Beechjet 400A known as the Model 400T, designated by the Air Force as the T-1A Jayhawk.

The service would use the T-1A to train future pilots to fly aerial refueling tankers such as the Boeing KC-135R and Lockheed C-5B Galaxy heavy lift transports. Including options, the contract called for up to 180 airplanes worth nearly $1 billion. First deliveries of the T-1A began in January, 1992.

Commercial Beechjet 400A and U.S. Air Force T1-A Jayhawk are shown on the production line at Beechcraft Wichita facilities.

On March 1, 1990, the second-generation Model 1900D regional airliner made its first flight. The latest version of Beechcraft's popular 19-seat, turboprop transport featured a stand-up cabin height of 71 inches, compared with 57 inches for the Model 1900C-1.

Certified one year later, the first production 1900D was delivered to Mesa Airlines in late November. The Farmington, New Mexico-based airline ordered 58 1900Ds, with the last to be delivered in 1996.

Other improvements found in the 1900D included a higher zero fuel weight and a maximum takeoff gross weight of 16,950 lb.—350 lb. more than its predecessor. Winglets and strakes mounted beneath the tail section improved both hot-day/high altitude performance and increased stability without the need for a complex stability augmentation system. Beech had produced 257 Model 1900 aircraft before production of the advanced 1900D began.

In 1991, international sales were strong despite tensions caused by the Persian Gulf War with Iraq. The Beechjet 400A, Model 350 Super King Air and other King Airs found a growing number of overseas customers.

The Model 300 LW, a lightweight version of the airplane limited to a maximum gross weight of 12,500 lb. for the European market, enjoyed increased acceptance along with the Model 200 Super King Air and Model C90A. Companies in France, Germany, Venezuela, Angola and Japan were a few of the Beechcraft customers that took delivery of King Airs.

Piston-powered aircraft sales continued to be successful, particularly as pilot training airplanes. Twelve specially-equipped Model A36 Bonanzas were delivered to Lufthansa Airlines, 23 A36 airplanes to Japan Airlines and 32 A36 aircraft to the Japan Civil Aviation College. Production of piston-powered Beechcrafts in 1991 totaled 241 airplanes, including 205 Bonanzas and 36 Model 58 Barons.

Jack Braly became president of Beech Aircraft Corporation in March 1991, after Max E. Bleck was selected to serve as president of the Raytheon Company and became chairman and CEO of Beech Aircraft Corporation.

Bleck had been one of the company's most effective leaders. In addition to successfully completing the Starship program, he played a pivotal role in the company's selection to build the U.S. Air Force T-1A Jayhawk.

To meet swelling demand for commercial and military versions of the Beechjet, the company had begun a major expansion of its production facilities in late 1990 and completed the project in the summer of 1991. As quickly as the building was released for occupancy, Beechcrafters were busy assembling both versions of the jet in an effort to meet growing demand.

A major event of 1991 was the maiden flight of the first production T-1A Jayhawk on July 5, followed in August by an order from Japan's Air Self-Defense Force for nine Beechjet 400T aircraft. The jets, modified slightly from T-1A configuration to meet Japanese requirements, would be used in the Self-Defense Force's TC-X program to train transport as well as search and rescue pilots. In October 1991, the company introduced the improved Starship 2000A and the C90B—an upgraded version of the highly successful C90A business turboprop.The Starship 2000A featured a higher maximum takeoff gross weight of 14,900 lb., permitting one additional passenger to be carried in its more spacious, six-seat cabin and boosting range to 1,500 nautical miles with full fuel. The Starship also received Danish certification that month.

Beechcraft engineers created the C90B by completely redesigning the cabin interior with new seats, headliner and sidewalls as well as more rugged consoles and tables. To make the latest King Air's cabin even quieter than its predecessor, the C90B featured tuned dynamic vibration absorbers strategically mounted throughout the interior, working in concert with advanced sound absorbent and moisture-resistant materials to decrease noise.

New, dynamically-balanced, four-blade propellers were chosen for the airplane's Pratt & Whitney Canada PT6A-21 engines. The propellers were more than three inches shorter than those used on the C90A, primarily to provide more tip-to-fuselage clearance.

A propeller phasing system was incorporated to interact with the vibration dampers and further reduce sound levels. Other benefits of the new propeller system were improved short-field performance and a lower minimum single-engine control speed of 80 knots. Customer response to the C90B was swift, with nearly 50 percent of the 1992 production sold before the end of 1991.

In addition to the Starship 2000A and the C90B, the company also introduced an executive version of the 1900D airliner in October. With its stand-up cabin and optional mix of club and airline-type seating arrangement, the executive-oriented 1900D was aimed at corporations seeking to replace aging aircraft used for shuttling management personnel to outlying facilities.

Although building the best business airplanes in the world kept Beechcrafters busy throughout 1991 and into 1992, the company continued to demonstrate its expertise as a leading aerospace subcontractor. When the U.S. Air Force/McDonnell Douglas C-17 transport prototype made its first flight in October 1991, it flew with composite main and nose landing gear doors and large winglets produced by Beech Aircraft Corporation.

From Staggerwing to Starship, quality, value and excellence in design and performance have been the quintessential elements of Beechcraft airplanes for more than 60 years. As the company prepares to enter the 21st Century, the words of Walter H. Beech will ring as true in the future as they have in the past—"The World is Small When You Fly a Beechcraft."

The Beechcraft Lineage

MODEL 17R - 1932

Designed by Theodore A. Wells, the five-seat Model 17 biplane had negative stagger wing configuration providing the pilot with excellent visibility. Powered by a 420 hp Wright R-975-E2 engine, the aircraft's maximum speed was more than 200 mph. Faired, fixed main landing gear had electric motors that partially retracted the wheels when airborne. Navy N-9 airfoil section was chosen by Wells for low drag and high speed. Wing flaps were not installed, and an electrically-operated pitch trim system pivoted the entire empennage. Aircraft's color was insignia red with dark maroon scalloping. First flight was made on November 5, 1932, flown by William "Pete" Hill. A second Model 17R, virtually identical to the first, was delivered in July, 1933 to Loffland Brothers Co., Tulsa, Okla. (Refer to Appendix C, #1)

Rare view of Model 17R, c/n 2 after being modified with full-swiveling tailwheel. Photograph taken at Cessna Aircraft Company factory site on Franklin Road (Pawnee Avenue). (Courtesy Robert J. Pickett).

MODEL 17R - 1934

Delivered to Ethyl Corporation April 19, 1934, original Model 17R was modified to suit its new owner with new paint scheme, narrow-chord, drag-type flaps under upper wing panels that were very similar to those installed on Model A17F; wider main gear and full-swiveling tailwheel of the A17F, c/n 5. NC499N was destroyed in a weather-related crash on December 10, 1935 at Nunda, New York, killing pilot Dewey Noyes. (Courtesy Robert J. Pickett) (Refer to Appendix C, #2)

MODEL A17F - A17FS - 1934

Powered by a 690 hp Wright R-1820-F11 radial, the Model A17F was built for the Goodall Worsted Company and Sanford Mills of Sanford, Maine. Delivered May 30, 1934, Robert S. Fogg flew the ship until November, 1934 when it was sold to Howard Hughes. It was entered unsuccessfully in the 1937 and 1938 Bendix cross-country races by pilot Bob Perlick. The airplane was destroyed by fire near Glendale, California, in the late 1930s. Capable of 225 mph, NC12583 was a high performance flying machine for 1934. First A17F was c/n 5, built during February -March, 1934. Narrow-chord flaps were installed on upper wing panels, ailerons on lower panels. Gross weight: 5,200 pounds. Beech also built one A17FS, c/n 11, in November, 1934, equipped with a Wright R-1820-F3 of 710 hp and gross weight of 6,000 pounds. Airplane was flown by the Bureau of Air Commerce from 1934-1937 when it was dismantled. Jack Wasall and future Cessna Aircraft Company president Dwane L. Wallace performed much of the engineering tasks for the A17F and A17FS along with Ted Wells. (Refer to Appendix C, #3)

Informal view of A17F c/n 5, NC12583, after factory rollout. Dewey and Blanche Noyes at left, Olive Ann and Walter Beech at right.

Profile view of powerful, bullish Beechcraft Model A17F, 1934.

MODEL B17 SERIES - 1934-1936

In 1934, Beech introduced the Model B17 series that were the first Beechcrafts produced in quantity. Offered with a choice of four powerplants, B17 series featured retractable landing gear, Clark CYH airfoil, ailerons and drag flaps on lower wings. Most popular was B17L shown here with Walter Beech. Powered by 225 hp Jacobs L-4 radial, B17L had maximum speed of 175 mph, cruised at 150 mph and cost $8,000. 48 were delivered from 1934-1936. B17B featured 285 hp Jacobs L-5, B17E used 285 hp Wright R-760-E1 and B17R mounted 420 hp Wright R-975-E2/E3. Because of the R-975's high price, the B17R cost $14,500. Only one B17B (c/n 20), four B17E and 16 B17R were delivered. One SB17L on Edo 38-3430 floats (c/n 40, NC15402) was built, in September, 1935. B17R was available on Edo 39-4000 floats. One B17R (c/n 72, NC15817) impressed by military as UC-43H during World War Two.

Factory-fresh B17L, c/n 15, 225 hp Jacobs L-4, August, 1934.

Hollywood actor Walter Pidgeon and actress Myrna Loy resting on the wing of an SB17L. ➤

MODEL C17 SERIES - 1936-1937

The improved C17 replaced the B17 series in 1936. The C17B was powered by a 285 hp Jacobs L-5 engine and proved to be the most popular of the C17 series. Forty aircraft were built in 1936-1937. The C17R featured a 420 hp Wright R-975-E2/E3 powerplant and had a maximum speed of more than 200 mph and a gross weight of 3,195 pounds. A nearly stock Beechcraft C17R (c/n 77) won the prestigious Bendix cross-country race in 1936, flown by Louise Thaden and Blanche Noyes. They became the first women to win the event. Sixteen C17R were delivered. The C17L was powered by a 225 hp Jacobs L-4 radial engine, had a maximum speed of 175 mph, landed at 45 mph and costs $7,495. Only six C17L were delivered. The airplane illustrated here is C17L c/n 107, exported to New Zealand as ZK-AEU in November, 1936, and flown by the Auckland Aero Club. The C17E featured a 285 hp Wright R-760 engine and two were built, both in 1937, and sold to Japan Airways Co., Ltd. The sole SC17B (c/n 99, NC16440), was a Model 17 amphibian built in 1936. One C17R (c/n 82, NC16434), was impressed into military service during World War Two as a C-43E. (Refer to Appendix C, #4)

MODEL C17R - (NAVY JB-1)

Walter Beech built good airplanes, and it wasn't long before the military establishment took notice of the Model 17's performance and dependability. In 1936, the U.S. Navy ordered one C17R powered by a 420 hp Wright R-975 radial and designated it JB-1. It was the first military Beechcraft in the sense that it was painted and outfitted according to the Navy's requirements. Assigned BuNo 0801, the airplane featured a unique, sweeping paint scheme. Beech c/n was 115, completed in December, 1936.

MODEL D17 SERIES

In 1937, Beech introduced the Model D17 series incorporating major changes from the earlier B17/C17 airplanes. The fuselage was lengthened 13 5/16 inches, ailerons were relocated to the upper wings (flaps remained on lower wing panels), rib spacing was reduced to 6 1/2 inches, toe brakes were installed and a new, full cantilever empennage assembly was designed. Airfoil section changed to NACA 23012 series. Four versions were offered: D17A with 350 hp Wright R-760-E2, D17R powered by 420 hp Wright R-975-E3, D17S featuring 450 hp Pratt & Whitney R-985 and the D17W, a special racing model powered by a 600 hp supercharged, geared Pratt & Whitney R-985-SC-G radial (D17W did not receive Approved Type Certificate). 53 D17S, 10 D17A, 27 D17R and one D17W were delivered from 1937 -1942. D17S cost $16,490 in July, 1937, had a gross weight of 4,250 pounds and cruising speed of 202 mph. Model D17R, NC17082 (c/n 137) is illustrated. SD17S version fitted with Edo WA-4665 floats. One was delivered in 1937. 25 D17S impressed into military as C-43B; 13 D17R impressed as C-43A; one D17A impressed as C-43F. The Model D17S became a hallmark airplane for Beech Aircraft Corporation. It set the standard for high-performance, single-engine private aircraft in the late 1930s, served with distinction in World War Two and remains one of the most classic airplanes ever built.

SD17S on floats. Note ventral fin and optional paint scheme. ▼

First Model D17R, c/n 137, with ground-adjustable propeller.

420 hp D17R in camouflage paint scheme, August, 1939.

D17A, c/n 360, 350 hp Wright, for Brazilian Navy, November, 1939.

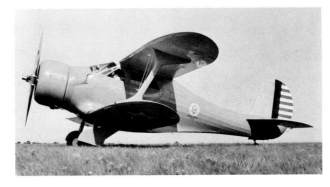

YC-43

Beech was awarded a U.S. Army contract in 1939 for three personnel transports, designated YC-43. Identical to the commercial D17S, the airplanes were assigned to air attache' duty in England, France and Italy. The three airplanes were: D17S c/n 295 (39-135) assigned to London, England; c/n 296 (39-140) assigned to Paris, France and c/n 297 (39-141) assigned to Rome, Italy. The first YC-43 is illustrated here, and was assigned to the U.S. Embassy in London. All three YC-43 were delivered in June, 1939.

GB-1

The U.S. Navy ordered seven D17S designated GB-1 in 1939 for use as personnel transports and general liason aircraft. Assigned to various shore stations across the nation, the seven GB-1 were: c/n 298 -304 (BuNo 1589 -1595). Exterior paint scheme was overall flat aluminum color except for black lettering/numbers and red/white/blue national insignia on wings. Beech delivered three additional GB-1 in 1940, c/n 385 - c/n 387 (BuNo 1898-1900).

UC-43

Beech built 105 C-43 and UC-43 personnel transports during World War Two for the U.S. Army Air Force. UC-43 illustrated was actually a U.S. Navy GB-1 (BuNo 01645) taken over by the U.S.A.A.F. and sent to China under the Army Defense Aid Program. Note landing lights under lower wing panels, ADF sensing loop under forward fuselage. Beech delivered 20 C/UC-43 in 1942, 79 in 1943, 3 in 1945. Unofficial name of C/UC-43 was "Traveler". Great Britain received 30 UC-43 designated Traveler Mk. I.

U.S.A.A.F UC-43 thunders through the sky on a Beech acceptance flight, 1943. Note two venturi tubes below fusleage for air-driven gyroscopic flight instruments.

MODEL D17S (GB-2)

After the attack on Pearl Harbor in December, 1941, Beech received large military orders for airplanes, including GB-2 general transports. Bascially identical to earlier GB-1, GB-2 series was painted in two-tone gray camouflage and all lettering was reduced in size. National insignia was applied to upper/lower wing surfaces and fuselage, but red circle in center of star was deleted. 310 GB-2 were built in World War Two. Performance same as commercial D17S. Beech delivered 23 GB-2 in 1941, 44 in 1942, 85 in 1943, 158 in 1944. Powered by Pratt & Whitney R-985-AN1 engine, GB-2 had maximum speed of 212 mph. GB-2 illustrated carries Beech c/n 4860 (1943 manufacture) on windows and cowling, navy BuNo 33061 on vertical stabilizer. Brazil received six airplanes in December, 1941, followed by eight additional ships in 1942. Great Britain received 75 GB-2 designated Traveler Mk. I under Lend-Lease from the U.S. Navy.

One of two D17S sent to China in 1937 equipped as air ambulance.

MODEL E17 SERIES

Introduced in 1937, the E17 series shared the long fuselage, upper wing ailerons and NACA 23012 airfoil of the D17 series but featured a semi-cantilever empennage. Two versions were offered: Model E17B powered by a 285 hp Jacobs L-5MB (magneto/battery ignition) radial and the E17L with 225 hp Jacobs L-4 engine. E17B illustrated (c/n 336) was sold to Indian National Airways, New Delhi, India in December, 1939. Model E17B cost $9,890 in 1937. 50 E17B were delivered from 1937 to 1940. Only one E17L (c/n 161) was built. Model E17B/E17L gross weight: 3,390 pounds. Maximum speed: E17B: 188 mph; E17L: 175 mph. 27 E17B were impressed into military service as C-43D during World War Two.

SE17B on skis. Note lack of gear doors, simple ski installation.

MODEL D17W (EXPERIMENTAL)

The first D17W was c/n 136, equipped with the experimental, supercharged/geared Pratt & Whitney R-985-SC-G of 600 hp. Pratt & Whitney did not market the powerplant and c/n 136 was re-engined with a 420 hp Wright R-975 and delivered as a D17R in October, 1936. In January, 1937, Jacqueline Cochran took delivery of D17W R18562 (c/n 164) and in July she set a speed record of 203.895 mph over a measured 1,000 kilometer course. In 1939 she set an altitude record of 30,052.43 feet over Palm Springs, California. With 600 hp available, the D17W's cruising speed at 13,500 feet was an impressive 235 mph. In 1942 the airplane entered military service, designated UC-43K.

MODEL F17D

The F17D was introduced in 1938 and featured the lengthened fuselage, upper wing ailerons, NACA 23012 airfoil, semi-cantilever empennage and 8-inch rib spacing of the E17 series. 56 were delivered from 1938-1940. Beech records indicate that four F17D were built after 1940: two in 1941 and two in April, 1942; c/n 412 and c/n 413, destined for the Defense Supply Corporation. A total of 61 F17D were produced. Powered by a 330 hp Jacobs L-6 radial, the F17D had a maximum speed of 185 mph and a gross weight of 3,590 pounds. 34 F17D were impressed into military service as C-43C during World War Two. F17D illustrated, PP-FAA (c/n 229) was built in August, 1938. Sold to Department de Aeronautica, Brazil.

Model D17S (UC-43) instrument panel was well equipped for 1943. Throttle is at center of panel with propeller control above and mixture directly below. Flap control switch is immediately above throttle. Fuel selectors are mounted on right cabin sidewall. Landing gear control is on lower panel. Vne (never exceed speed) on airspeed indicator is red-lined at 240 mph.

MODEL G17S

Beech offered the Model G17S in 1946 as the final variant of the majestic Staggerwing series. Major changes included a new engine cowling, slightly larger windshield, revised instrument panel layout and redesigned empennage surfaces. In January, 1946, Beech established a production schedule for at least 50 airplanes, but only 20 were built. Fifteen were built by Beech (c/n B-1 - B-15) and c/n B-20, a factory demonstrator. The remaining airplanes were assembled and sold by Henry Seale Aviation Co., Dallas, Tex. Priced at $29,000 with a new Pratt & Whitney R-985 engine, the G17S had a maximum speed of 212 mph at 5,500 feet. Gross weight was 4,250 pounds. The G17S illustrated is c/n B-1, originally delivered to Cuban Dominican Sales Co., in July, 1946. Beech records indicate a total of 785 Model 17 biplanes were manufactured from 1932 to 1948. (Refer to Appendix C, #5)

Comparison of U.S. Navy GB-2 (background) and postwar Model G17S exemplifies changes to windshield and cowling on the G17S. Registered NX21934, the airplane is Beech c/n 424, a D17S that was modified into the G17S prototype in 1945. Airplane was personal mount of none other than Walter H. Beech himself, as testified by his name painted on the cabin door.

Model G17S Instrument panel illustrates revised design that improved panel's appearance. Control wheel is very similar to that used on Model D18S of 1946. Note throw-over control column, orderly placement of instruments and switches.

In 1940, Beech engineers toyed with fighter/ground attack aircraft featuring negative stagger wing layout, 1090 hp Allison V-12 upright inline engine, 37 mm cannon firing through the propeller hub and a .30 caliber and .50 caliber machine gun firing through the propeller arc. Maximum speed was expected to be 350 mph. War production forced an end to development in 1941.

MODEL 18A - PROTOTYPE

Conceived by Walter H. Beech and Ted Wells, design work on the Beechcraft Model 18 began in December, 1935. Two 320 hp Wright R760-E2 radial engines powered the prototype airplane, c/n 62, NC15810. The Model 18A was both the first all-metal and the first multi-engine Beech airplane produced. Wing used NACA 23018 airfoil at root, changed to NACA 23012 outboard of nacelles to tips. Ailerons, rudder and elevator were metal with fabric cover. Plain flaps on underside of wings were electrically operated. Conventional landing gear extended and retracted electrically. Small blisters on cowlings provided clearance for engine rocker boxes and reduced drag. Model 18A first flight: January 15, 1937. Pilot: James N. Peyton, a TWA pilot employed to do initial flight testing because of his experience with multi-engine airplanes; co-pilot: H.C. Rankin (Beech test pilot); flight test engineer: Robert Johnson, an employee of Curtiss-Wright Corporation. The Ethyl Corporation, who purchased the first Model 17R, also purchased the first Model 18, taking delivery in June, 1937. The prototype is illustrated soon after completion in January, 1937. Note "NC" registration despite the fact that no Approved Type Certificate had been issued and flight testing was just beginning. Registration was changed to "NX15810" soon after this photograph was taken.(Refer to Appendix C, #6)

Designer Ted Wells poses with first Model 18, c/n 62, NC15810.

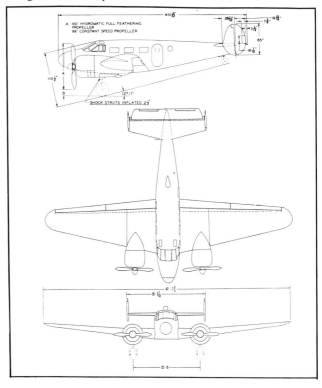

Instrument panel of Model 18A prototype, c/n 62, NC15810. Layout was spartan but functional. Panel and control wheels are very similar to earlier Model 17 series.

MODEL 18A

Starratt Airways of Hudson, Ontario, Canada bought the first production airplane, a Model S18A capable of operating on floats or skis. Beechcraft's twin was a rugged, dependable and very versatile aircraft. Powered with two, 320 hp Wright R-760 engines swinging constant-speed propellers, CF-BGY operated year round in the Canadian bush country. Six Model 18 were built in 1937; one Model S18A, one Model 18A, two Model 18B, one S18B and one Model S18D rebuilt from Model S18A. Maximum speed of Model 18A was 202 mph; gross weight 6,500 pounds and cost $37,500. S18A of Starratt Airways is illustrated on floats.

MODEL 18B - Model 18D

By 1938 the Beechcraft Model 18 was offered with three powerplants: Model 18A: 320 hp Wright R-760-E2; Model 18B: 285 hp Jacobs L-5; Model 18D: 330 hp Jacobs L-6. The L-6 engine was new and made the Model 18D attractive to customers who didn't want the lower horsepower Model 18A or 18B. The first production Model 18D was c/n 175, built in May, 1938. Except for engine installation, the Model 18A, 18B and 18D shared the same airframe. Gross weight varied from 6,500 pounds for the Model 18A to 7,200 pounds for Model 18D. Model S18D illustrated, CF-BKO, (c/n 178) was one of two S18D delivered to Prairie Airways, Ltd. of Moose Jaw, Saskatchewan, Canada in 1938. Interior fabrics and colors of early production Model 18s were often selected by Olive Ann Beech.

MODEL 18S

Ted Wells and Dean E. Burleigh started development of the Model 18S in August, 1938 and the first example, c/n 222, NC19452 was completed in January, 1939. Powered by two 450 hp Pratt & Whitney "Wasp Jr." engines, the prototype Beechcraft Model 18S won the Macfadden Trophy race in January, 1940. Flown by H.C. Rankin and Walter H. Beech, NC19452 flew from St. Louis to Miami in 4 hours, 37 minutes at an average speed of more than 234 mph. Model 18S mated Beechcraft Model 18's rugged airframe to Pratt & Whitney's dependable R-985 radial engine, creating a winning combination. Maximum speed was 240 mph; gross weight: 7,200 pounds. Price was $63,500 in November, 1940. 18S prototype illustrated also was used as a testbed for developing unique cupola installation on the U.S. Navy JRB-1 of 1940. It was converted to 18S configuration and sold to Olson Drilling Company of Tulsa, Oklahoma in June, 1940. Model 18S-series airplanes featured larger vertical stabilizer/rudder required by higher horsepower and gross weight increase with R-985 intallation. (Courtesy Joseph P. Juptner)

◄ F-2/F-2B

In 1940 the U.S. Army Air Corps ordered 14 Model 18S for high altitude photographic work. Designated F-2, Beech constructor numbers were c/n 340 -c/n 353. The first ship was delivered in December, 1939 and the last airplane in July, 1940. Army serial numbers were 40-682- 40-695. The interior was custom-designed to accept a variety of camera installations, including equipment for night photography. A special door was installed in the entry door permitting side-view or oblique-angle photography. Engines were Pratt & Whitney R-985-14, 450 horsepower. F-2 regularly flew at 25,000 feet on photographic missions and was fully equipped with supplemental oxygen system. The first military Beechcraft Model 18 was not the F-2 but c/n 223, a Model 18D sold to the Philippine Army Air Corps in March, 1939. However, the U.S. Army's success and satisfaction with the F-2's performance paved the way for thousands of military Beechcraft airplanes in World War Two. U.S. Army eventually bought 56 F-2 series, including the F-2A with R-985-AN3 engines and F-2B with R-985-AN1. F-2B model was equivalent to U.S.A.A.F. AT-11A.

MODEL 18R (SWEDEN)

The Swedish Royal Air Force ordered one (c/n 321) Beechcraft Model 18R in late 1939 to be specially outfitted as an aerial ambulance. Designed to accept floats or skis, the airplane was delivered in January, 1940 to Kungl Flygfoervaltningen (SRAF) and shipped by sea to Sweden. Powered by Wright R-975 radial engines, the Model 18R was also ordered by the Republic of China in 1940. Designated AT18R, six airplanes (c/n 375 - c/n 380) were delivered, equipped with bomb racks, provision for fixed and flexible machine guns and room for a bombardier in the nose section.

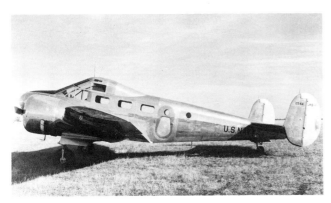

JRB-1

In 1940, the U.S. Navy ordered five JRB-1, outfitted with a special cupola above the cockpit for an observer who controlled aerial target drones. Beech modified the first Model 18S (c/n 222 licensed as NX19452 for experimental flight testing) with a sheet metal cupola structure. Five Navy airplanes were c/n 425 - c/n 429, BuNo 2543 -2547. All delivered in late 1940. Gross weight was 8,727 pounds. Powered by Pratt & Whitney R-985-AN-4 or -50 engines, the JRB-1 had a maximum speed of 225 mph. Beech also built over 300 JRB-3 and JRB-4 personnel transports for the U.S. Navy in 1944-1945 that were equivalent to Army C-45F transport.

First JRB-1 for U.S. Navy (c/n 425), October, 1941.

C/UC-45B

In 1940, the U.S. Army Air Corps ordered 11 Beechcraft Model 18S designated C-45 for use as general duty light transports. Painted with blue fuselage and chrome yellow wings, the first airplane was delivered in March, 1940 and the last airplane in August. Beech constructor numbers were c/n 364 - c/n 374, Army serial numbers 40-180 -40-190. After Pearl Harbor in December, 1941, Beech received contracts for thousands of airplanes and eventually built over 1,400 C/UC-45 for the U.S.A.A.F. All were based on the commercial C18S. UC-45B illustrated is Army s/n 43-35448, Beech c/n 5980. Engines were 450 hp Pratt & Whitney R-985-AN-1 or AN-3. Postwar derivatives of the C-45 series were: C-45G, TC-45G, C-45H, TC-45H, TC-45J, UC-45J, RC-45J. Great Britain received C-45 under Lend-Lease designated "Expeditor I" and "Expeditor II". The U.S. Air Force retired its last C-45s in November, 1963, after 20 years of service. Unofficial name for C-45 series was "Expeditor".

Wartime shortages forced the temporary use of wooden wheels on many C-45 transports rolling off the assembly lines. The aircraft were stored outside until conventional wheels and tires became available. (Courtesy Jim Horne collection)

Instrument panel of UC-45B is typical of wartime C-45 series. Rudder pedals are equipped with toe brakes, autopilot in left side of panel has integral heading and attitude indicators. Throttles are in center of console, propeller controls at left, mixture controls at right.

C/UC-45F

Beech continued to produce the C/UC-45 series into 1945. C-45F illustrated was built late in the war and bears Beech c/n 7870 on fuselage and nose. Army s/n is 44-47462. Fuel capacity was 206 gallons, maximum speed 215 mph. C-45F could carry five passengers and two pilots in comfort, plus 80 pounds of baggage. Engines were 450 hp Pratt & Whitney R-985-AN-1 or AN-3. Army C-45F were equivalent to U.S. Navy JRB-3 - JRB-4 personnel transports.

SNB-1

Ordered by the U.S. Navy in 1941, the SNB-1 was designed to train gunner and bombardier personnel and was equivalent to the Army's AT-11. First production batch of 14 airplanes were built in August, 1942 and were part of the 73 total accepted by the Navy that year. 247 SNB-1 were built in 1943, when production was terminated. Machine gun turret was electrically operated. SNB-1 used turrets built by Beech and Crocker-Wheeler that mounted twin .30-caliber weapons. Bomb racks were built into the lower fuselage aft of the front spar and accomodated up to ten 100-pound bombs. 320 SNB-1 were accepted for service by the Navy during World War Two. Aircraft illustrated is c/n 4441, built in 1943. Beech adopted a thousand-series constructor number system in 1941 that was used throughout the war. SNB-1 was powered by 450 hp Pratt & Whitney R-985-AN1. Gross weight was 9,300 pounds.

SNB-2

Beech started producing the SNB-2 version in July, 1942, when 4 were built. The SNB-2 was utilized primarily as a navigation trainer and general purpose transport. Aircraft illustrated served the Air Force, Atlantic Fleet on the east coast of the United States. Photograph was taken at Norfolk Naval Air Station, Norfolk, Virginia. Navy PB4Y-1 in background was probably assigned to anti-submarine duty along the coast. SNB-2 was powered by Pratt & Whitney R-985-25 engines of 450 hp. Maximum speed: 225 mph; gross weight: 8,700 pounds. The U.S. Navy took delivery of 606 SNB-2 during the war. Deliveries began in 1942 with 44 airplanes, peaked at 286 in 1943. 276 were delivered in 1944.

SNB-4/SNB-5/SNB-5P

The U.S. Navy returned 117 SNB-1 personnel transports to the Beech factory in 1947 for rebuilding and modification that completely refurbished the war-weary fleet. Each airplane was disassembled, inspected and reassembled with new parts and assemblies as required. When completed the airplanes were re-designated SNB-4 by the Navy and continued their role as navigation and general transport aircraft. In 1951, a refurbishing program began at Beech's Herington, Kansas facility for U.S. Navy SNB-series airplanes. New, stronger wing center section truss assemblies and disc-type wheel brakes were installed. Hamilton-Standard "Hydromatic" constant-speed, full-feathering propellers were mounted and the engine nacelles were lengthened and streamlined aft above the wing. Major changes to the cockpit included new instrumentation for both pilot and co-pilot and installation of Sperry autopilots. The many changes and improvements brought the airplanes up to commercial D18S configuration. Designated SNB-5P by the U.S. Navy, a total of 2,263 airplanes were modified by Beech during the 10-year program. SNB-5P illustrated is fresh from Beech's Herington modification center.

C-45G/C-45H

The U.S. Air Force returned many war-weary C-45, AT-7 and AT-11 airplanes to Beech for complete overhaul and modification to the same Model D18S standards as the U.S. Navy SNB-5P, including heavier wing center section truss structure, new landing gear struts, wheels and brakes, instrument panel and avionics/instrumentation. USAF aircraft seated six and featured Hamilton Standard two-blade, constant-speed, full-feathering propellers as part of the refitting program. Majority of work was accomplished at the Herington, Kansas facility from 1951 to 1961. USAF C-45H illustrated is ready for delivery. Beech's rebuilding program for the U.S. Navy and Air Force gave military Model 18s a second life and many soldiered on until the early 1960s before being replaced by more modern aircraft.

AT-7

Beech designed the AT-7 to meet a U.S. Army Air Force requirement for a navigation trainer. Equipment included drift meters, work tables and compasses in the cabin. An auxiliary instrument panel with essential flight/navigation instrumentation was mounted in the front of the cabin for student reference. Celestial navigation sightings were made through a small turret in cabin roof. Thousands of navigators graduated from the AT-7 to B-17s and B-24s. 187 AT-7 were delivered in 1941; peak production occurred in 1943 when 361 airplanes went to war. A total of 884 AT-7 were accepted by the Army during World War Two. Powered by 450 hp Pratt & Whitney R-985-25 engines, AT-7 had a maximum speed of 225 mph, cruised at 190 mph. Gross weight: 8,727 pounds. AT-7 illustrated was completed in September, 1943. AT-7 was also designated T-7-BH. Beech records indicate 19 AT-7 were built as UC-45 series in 1943 for use as Army personnel transports. Unofficial name for AT-7 was "Navigator".

With gear retracted and cowl flaps closed, a Beechcraft for the U.S. Army Air Force rips through the Kansas skies on a test flight in January, 1942. (Jim Horne collection).

April, 1944 photograph of U.S.A.A.F. AT-7 navigation trainer.

AT-7A - AT-7B - AT-7C

The versatile AT-7 was designated AT-7A when modified to accept floats and skis. One airplane was modified with float and ski fittings in August, 1943, 12 in September and 30 more were built in October with the same modifications. Two 450 hp Pratt & Whitney R-985-AN1 engines gave the AT-7A a maximum speed of 210 mph, cruise of 174 mph. AT-7A illustrated on beaching gear with entry door open and special boarding ladder deployed. Large ventral fin under aft fuselage provided additional vertical area for directional stability with floats installed. Airplane is c/n 1176, Army s/n 41-21161 used to test float installation. Photograph taken on November 23, 1942. AT-7B variant featured special cold-climate equipment for possible sub-zero temperature operations and 450 hp R-985-25 engines. AT-7C had a more complex and sophisticated avionics/autopilot than AT-7/AT-7A/AT-7B, was fitted with 450 hp R-985-AN-3 engines. AT-7C also designated T-7C-BH by the Army. ▼

AT-7 trainer photographed January 2, 1942. Note rudder stripes. This airplane became the testbed for AT-7A float version. Turret above fuselage was used for training students in principles of celestial navigation.

24

AT-11 - AT-11A

Beech's AT-11 taught thousands of young men to say "Bomb's away!", dropping lethal high explosives on America's adversaries with devastating accuracy. AT-11s were based primarily in the southwestern United States where favorable flying weather prevailed and made almost round-the-clock training possible. Equipped with bombsights and racks holding up to ten 100-pound practice bombs, the AT-11 normally carried three students and a crew of two on training missions. A clear plexiglass nose dome housed the famed Norden bombsight. Some AT-11 were converted to navigation trainers similar to AT-7 series, but most were dedicated to bombardier training. Deliveries began in December, 1941 and 1,560 were delivered to the U.S. Army Air Force during the war. Peak production reached 749 airplanes in 1942. Beech delivered the last production AT-11 in May, 1944. Model AT-11 also designated T-11-BH. AT-11A was basic AT-11 modified for aerial photography missions. Beech built 42 F-2B versions that were equivalent to AT-11A. AT-11/AT-11A powered by 450 hp Pratt & Whitney R-985-AN1 or -AN3. Maximum speed: 215 mph. Gross weight: 9,300 pounds. AT-11 illustrated was completed in August, 1941 and displays its unique "bomber nose" section where student bombardiers learned their deadly trade. Aircraft is U.S.A.A.C. serial number 41-9437. Many AT-11s were converted to C-45G/C-45H configuration between 1951-1961. Unofficial name of AT-11 was "Kansan".

Profile view of U.S. Army Air Corps AT-11 bombardier trainer, built in August, 1941. Note red/white/blue rudder stripes that quickly disappeared after America's entry into World War Two.

Oblique view of AT-7A on floats with beaching gear.

"Acres of Beechcraft." Final assembly seemingly stretches to infinity. Believed to be a composite photo. U.S. Army AT-11 and Navy SNB-1 production line in December, 1941. Note pre-war red-white-blue rudder stripes. (Jim Horne collection). ▼

Model D18S owned by Hollywood's 20th Century Fox, August, 1946.

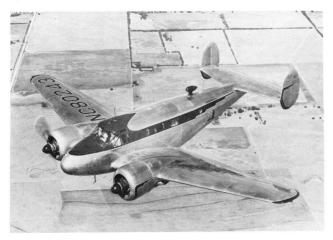

Cockpit view of Model D18S instrument panel.

MODEL C18S/D18S

In late 1944, Beech produced a small number of commercial Model C18S airplanes that were equivalent to the Army C-45F and Navy JRB-4 personnel transports. Originally designed in 1940, the C18S had minor structural changes from the Model B18S. Beech records indicate one C18S (c/n 432) was delivered to the Philippine Army Air Corps in November, 1940. C18S was the basic airframe used to build U.S.A.A.F. UC-45 -AT-7 -AT-11 series and Navy SNB -JRB series in World War Two. Engines were Pratt & Whitney R-985, 450 hp. When hostilities ended in August, 1945, Beech introduced the postwar Model D18S, very similar to the C18S but featuring longer, more streamlined engine nacelles and a stronger wing center section structure that permitted a gross weight of 8,500 pounds or 8,750 if Hamilton Standard Hydromatic propellers were installed (later modifications allowed a gross weight of 9,000 pounds). The cabin accomodated six to nine people in comfort. 296 D18S were produced in 1946...the highest number for any Model 18 in a single year. Beech introduced a new constructor number system after the war that assigned separate c/n for each model Beechcraft. D18S were designated by the letter "A" followed by the c/n. Records indicate that over 1,000 D18S were produced from 1945-1955. Powered by Pratt & Whitney R-985-series engines, the D18S had a maximum speed of 230 mph at 5,000 feet and cost $61,500 for the basic airplane. In 1951, Beech started production on the first of 283 "Canadian Expeditor" D18S for the Royal Canadian Air Force (RCAF). Designated Mk. 3N, Mk. 3NM and Mk. 3TM (desginated later as Mk. 3T, Mk.3TM, Mk. 3NMT) the airplanes were employed as communications and navigation trainers. Performance was basically identical to commercial D18S. D18S illustrated was owned by Hollywood's Twentieth Century Fox Studios.

Factory-fresh Model D18S ready for delivery.

Time Magazine purchased this specially-equipped Model C18S in October, 1945 for photographic and transport work. Airplane is fitted with door-mounted access panel for oblique photography that is identical to panels used on F-2 and other Beech military Model 18 derivatives. A lavatory was installed in the aft cabin.

MODEL D18C/CT

One of the most rare of all Twin Beech versions, development of the 1946 Model 18CT was inspired by the promising postwar feeder airline market. Designed to seat 8-9 passengers, primary change from the Model D18S was three-fold: two Continental R-9A, nine-cylinder radial engines rated at 525 hp for takeoff and 500 hp at 2300 rpm for climb and cruise were installed on the 18C and 18CT; the D18CT was designed specifically as a small airliner and featured extra safety equipment as required with the interior outfitted accordingly; the 18CT was certified under the stringent rules of Civil Aeronautics Authority Section 04 requiring additional structural integrity and rigorous testing before certification while the 18C was intended for executive service with custom-designed interiors and certified under CAR Section 03. Standard maximum gross weight was 9,000 pounds but optional gross weight of 9,450 pounds was permitted if Hamilton Standard Hydromatic, full-

feathering propellers were installed. R-9A engine was a new development in 1946, and Beech contracted to receive some of the earliest examples for use on the D18C/CT. Cruising speed was 224 mph (75% power setting) at 8,500 feet and maximum speed was 240 mph at 3,900 feet. Standard fuel capacity: 206 gallons with 47-gallon auxiliary tank optional (253 gallons total); range was 900 statute miles with 253 gallons of fuel. The D18C cost $64,250 and the D18CT (airliner configuration) cost $64,887 fly away factory (FAF). According to Beech production records, only 29 D18C/CT were built and delivered, but FAA records show 31 airplanes produced, starting with c/n AA-1 and ending with c/n AA-31. Of these, 16 were built as D18CT for feeder airline service. First deliveries occurred in April, 1946. ATC 765 granted D18C on 7-16-47; ATC 770 granted D18CT on 6-3-47. Model D18CT in the livery of Inland Airways is illustrated. (Courtesy Joseph P. Juptner)

MODEL SUPER E18S ➤

Introduced in the fall of 1954, the Model E18S was the first of Beech's Super 18 series and incorporated many changes. The most salient were: cabin height raised six inches for increased head room, four cabin windows, larger airstair-type cabin door, gross weight of 9,300 pounds, wingspan increased four feet to 49 feet eight inches (increase of 12 square feet of area to 361 square feet), new wing tips that provided increased single-engine climb rate and service ceiling. Pratt & Whitney R-985-series radial engines of 450 hp were installed. E18S was produced from August, 1954 until January, 1960 when it was replaced by the Model G18S. Records indicate 451 Model E18S were delivered from 1954 to 1960. Cruising speed for the E18S was 215 mph at 10,000 feet. E18S illustrated has landing lights in nose cap, custom paint scheme. Model E18S-9700 had three-blade Hartzell propellers and a gross weight of 9,700 pounds. Model E18S c/n have a "BA" prefix.

Model E18S instrument panel displays throttle, mixture and propeller levers featuring shaped knobs for easy identification, landing gear and flap controls located in center pedestal.

MODEL SUPER G18S

Beechcraft's Model 18 was 22 years old in 1959, but it continued to be in demand as a business and executive airplane largely because of its solid performance, dependability and investment value. Customer deliveries of the improved Model G18S began in December, 1959. The only major changes were an increase in gross weight to 9,700 pounds, three-blade Hartzell propellers and a new, two-piece windshield that improved the airplane's appearance and diffusion of rain. Minor change was a large, center cabin window that increased passenger viewing area. A total of 154 G18S were delivered from 1959-1963. 1961 G18S is illustrated.

MODEL SUPER H18

1962 marked the 25th year of continuous Model 18 production. In August, Beech introduced the Model Super H18, the last version of a truly great airplane. Gross weight was 9,900 pounds, useful load reached an all-time high of more than 4,200 pounds and maximum speed was 236 mph. The landing gear struts featured half-fork design instead of the full-fork used on previous models and smaller 8.50 x 10 wheels/tires were installed. Electric cowl flaps were standard and air conditioning was available for the first time in a Model 18. Lightweight, three-blade propellers were

standard and the main fuel tank capacity was increased to 99 gallons. In 1963, Beech offered a choice of landing gear configurations; customers could order the standard, conventional gear version or the Volpar-designed tricycle gear installation that was installed at the Beech factory. Eventually, only the tricycle-gear model was built. The last of nearly 8,000 Beechcraft Model 18s were delivered on November 26, 1969 when three Model Super H18 departed Beech Field for Japan, to be used by Japan Air Lines as multi-engine pilot trainers. A total of 149 H18 were produced from 1963-1970. (Refer to Appendix C, #7)

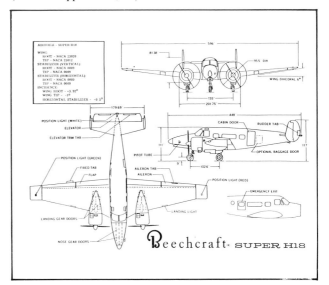

Instrument panel of Model Super H18 shows autopilot mode controller, weather radar installation. Panel had ample room for modern avionics equipment.

Beech considered construction of the Model 20M twin-engine version of the Model 17 in mid-1937, powered by two Menasco C6S4 Super Buccaneer, inverted, liquid-cooled 6-cylinder powerplants developing 260 hp each at 2300 rpm. Maximum speed was expected to be 240 mph, gross weight 4,850 pounds, range of 600 statute miles. Wingspan: 32 feet; length: 26 feet 9 inches. The Model 18 took precedence over the Model 20M; development ceased in 1938. ►

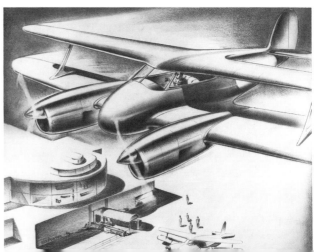

MODEL 23 MUSKETEER (PROTOTYPE)

Beech Aircraft Corporation entered the light, single-engine market in 1963 with the Model 23 Musketeer. Designed and developed at Wichita, the prototype Model 23 made its first flight 10-23-61 with S.C. Tuttle at the controls. Soon after the maiden flight, full-swiveling nose gear unit was moved forward and first flew on December 19, 1961. John I. Elliot was chief project engineer on the Model 23, which took advantage of Beech's manufacturing experience with truss-grid, honeycomb core material used to build control surfaces for the Convair F-106 jet fighter. The laminar flow wing used honeycomb ribs bonded to the external skin for drag reduction and strength. Musketeer prototype N948B is illustrated with nose gear in original, aft location.

MODEL 23 MUSKETEER

Beechcraft's new Musketeer featured trailing beam-type, tricycle landing gear and room for four occupants in a cabin surrounded with generous window area. Large, aft-curving windshield permitted excellent pilot visibility in all directions. Production Musketeers had the nose gear unit located further forward than prototype and the gear was made steerable through the rudder pedals to improve ground handling characteristics. Fuel capacity totalled 60 gallons, maximum gross weight was 2,300 pounds. Maximum speed 144 mph with a maximum range of 873 statute miles at 65% power setting. Powered by a four-cylinder, 160 hp Lycoming 0-320-D2B opposed engine, Model 23 sold for $13,300 including a single radio and complete flight instrumentation. Initial deliveries began in October, 1962 from the Wichita factory. 553 were produced in the 1963 model year. Note baggage door located on right side of fuselage.

MODEL A23-A23A-A23-24

Beech introduced the improved Model A23 Musketeer II in June, 1964 that featured a third cabin window, 165 hp fuel-injected Lycoming engine and minor interior/exterior refinements to enhance customer appeal. Price was $14,250. 346 Musketeer II were built, followed in 1965 by the new Musketeer III series that offered three different airplanes: 150 hp Sport III ($11,500); 165 hp Custom III ($14,950) and 200 hp Super III ($16,350). The four-place Model A23-24 Musketeer Super III first flew 11-19-65. Powered by a 200 hp Lycoming IO-360-A2B engine equipped with a two-blade, fixed-pitch propeller, maximum speed was 158 mph and normal category gross weight was 2,550 pounds. The Model A23A Musketeer Custom III used Lycoming's IO-346-A engine producing 165 hp at 2700 rpm and seated four. Model A23A first flight was 10-15-65. In 1966, Beech offered the six-seat Musketeer Custom III powered by a 180 hp Lycoming O-360-A2G. Maximum speed was 151 mph with a 860 statute mile range with 45 minute reserve. Model A23, A23A and A23-24 were produced at Beech's Liberal, Kansas facility that began manufacturing operations exclusively for the Musketeer series in June, 1964. Beech offered an optional left side cabin door on all models. Only the right door was standard. A 1966 Model A23-24 Musketeer Custom III is illustrated.

Musketeer instrument panel was well equipped for 1966 with dual nav/com radios, ADF, gyroscopic flight instruments and exhaust gas temperature (EGT) system.

MODEL A23-19 SPORT/MODEL B19 SPORT 150

Beech introduced the two-place, Model A23-19 Sport in 1965 as an economy version of the A23-series used for basic flight training. Powered by a 150 hp Lycoming 0-320-E2C series engine, the A23-19 had a maximum speed of 140 mph and a gross weight of 2,250 pounds. Only two cabin windows were installed, reminiscent of the early Model 23 Musketeer. In 1968 the Model 19A Musketeer Sport III aerobatic version was offered, delivered with g-meter, quick-release right-side door and shoulder harnesses as standard equipment. In 1969, the Musketeer Custom III received an aerobatic version with a 180 hp Lycoming engine. The Model B19 debuted in 1970 followed in 1972 by the B-19 Sport 150, both with 150 hp Lycoming powerplants. Production of the Model A23/19/19A/M19A/B19 occurred from 1966 to 1978 and totalled 1,525 airplanes. Model B19 Sport 150 is illustrated.

MODEL A24R/B24R/C24R

In 1970, Beech engineers designed the Model A24R Super R featuring an electro-hydraulic, retractable landing gear system. Main gear retracted outward into large recesses while the nose gear rotated 90 degress to lay flat in its well. A Lycoming IO-360-A1B, fuel-injected engine developing 200 hp at 2700 rpm powered the A24R to a cruising speed of 162 mph at 7,500 feet. 60 gallons of fuel permitted a range of 711 statute miles at 75% power setting. Price was $24,950. In 1972, Beech introduced the B24R, named "Sierra 200" with standard left side cabin door and built 55 airplanes that year. The B24R featured system and interior refinements, including a 1 1/2-inch lower instrument panel and improved IO-360-A2B engine with counter-weighted crankshaft, relocated oil cooler (firewall). Built from 1973 to 1976, 299 B24R were produced. In 1977, the C24R Sierra 200 entered production beginning with c/n MC-499 and continuing through MC-795 for a total of 345 airplanes. C24 featured fairings to reduce drag around main gear, aileron gap seals and improved, more efficient propeller that gave a six-knot increase in speed and higher service ceiling. C24R illustrated banks away to show retracted gear.

MODEL B23/C23

The 1966 Model A23A Musketeer Custom III evolved into the Model B23 Musketeer Custom III of 1968 and Model C23 of 1970. Major changes for the 1970 model year included a wider front cabin (4 1/2 inches added at the two front seats) and larger, reshaped cabin windows. Two windows were standard on the B19 Sport, three on the Custom and Super models while the Super could add a fourth window when the optional third seat was ordered (making the Musketeer Super a six-seat airplane). First C23 was c/n M-1285 and continued through M-1361 in 1971. Seating four, the C23 received a 180 hp Lycoming 0-360-A4G engine in 1972 and featured a standard left side door. Renamed Sundowner 180, maximum cruising speed was 143 mph and gross weight 2,450 pounds. The first production Sundowner 180 was c/n M-1362 and the last was M-2392, built in 1983. The instrument panel on the 1973 Sport and Sundowner was lowered 1 1/2 inches for improved forward visibility and the throttle, mixture and carburetor heat controls were mounted in a new quadrant. Only significant change for 1974 was a one inch increase in window height. Late-model C23 series (1975-1983) have Avco Lycoming 0-360-A2G, 0-360-A4G, 0-360-A4J or 0-360-A4K engines developing 180 hp at 2700 rpm. Model C23 Sundowner 180 illustrated has optional heated pitot tube on left wing, Beech Aero Club insignia on wing and tail.

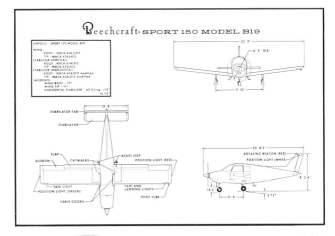

1977 Sundowner instrument panel features digital display nav/comm avionics, transponder and complete instrumentation for IFR flight.

MODEL 25/26 WICHITA

Designed by Beech engineers under the supervision of Ted Wells, the Beechcraft Model 25 answered the U.S. Army's need for an advanced multi-engine pilot trainer that could be built with non-strategic materials, primarily wood. Development began in early 1940 and cost $255,000. The prototype crashed and burned on May 5, 1941 during army tests. Undaunted, Beech initiated design work for the followup Model 26 on May 6, 1941. On July 19 the new AT-10 made its first flight with Beech test pilot H.C. "Ding" Rankin and co-pilot John P. Gaty at the controls. Deliveries began in February, 1942 and 748 were manufactured that year. Beech production ceased in 1943 after a total of 1,771 AT-10 were built.

The Globe Aircraft Corporation produced 600 ships before terminating production in 1944 for a total of 2,371 AT-10 built in World War Two. Majority of fuselage and wings were constructed of plywood with sheet aluminum used only in the cockpit/nose sections, nacelles and cowlings. Subcontractors provided majority of AT-10 parts, components and subassemblies because they could be manufactured by relatively unskilled labor. Powered by two 290 hp Lycoming R-680-9 radial engines with two-blade, constant-speed propellers, AT-10 had a maximum speed of 190 mph. Cockpit canopy slid aft for entry/exit. AT-10 served alongside Cessna's AT-17 "Bobcat" advanced pilot trainer, also designed to the same basic specifications, during the war.

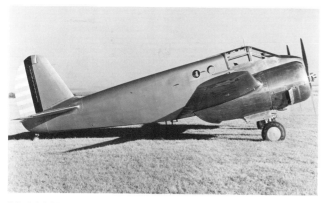

Model 26/AT-10, second prototype built, November, 1941. Wood fuselage was covered by doped fabric.

AT-10 "Wichita" advanced multi-engine trainers await students.

Early production AT-10 advanced, multi-engine trainers fly in formation. Beech produced a total of 1,771 AT-10s during the war. (Jim Horne collection).

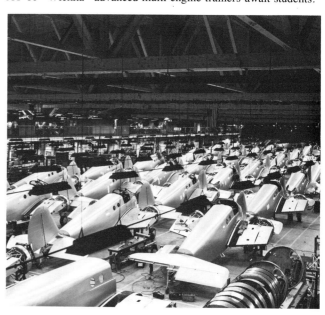

View of busy Beechcraft assembly line shows a portion of the 1,771 AT-10 trainers produced from 1941 to 1943. (Jim Horne collection).

MODEL 28

Beechcraft's Model 28 was designed as a ground attack aircraft capable of delivering knock-out blows to fortified gun emplacements, armored vehicles and coastal surface vessels. A hand-picked engineering team led by Bill Cassidy began development in 1943, and the first airplane flew on May 7, 1944 with Beech test pilot Vern Carstens at the wheel. The Model 28 was not a modified Model 18 but a totally new design. Designated XA-38 "Grizzly" by the U.S. Army Air Force (but also known as the "Destroyer" at Beech), a 75 mm Type T15E1 automatic cannon with 20 rounds was mounted in the nose. Aiming the cannon was simple: point the airplane at the target and fire. Sighting was aided by a Type N-6 reflector unit. Six .50-caliber machine guns complemented the cannon's firepower. Four were located in twin,

remote-control turrets and two more in the lower nose section. A gunner controlled the turrets but the pilot could fire the lower turret and nose guns plus the cannon simultaneously if desired. Two, 2,300 hp Wright Duplex "Cyclone" GR-3350-43 18-cylinder, twin-row radial engines powered the XA-38 to a maximum speed of 331 mph at sea level. Basic gross weight was 29,900 pounds with a combat gross weight (with ordnance) of 36,332 pounds. Fuel capacity was 825 gallons in self-sealing tanks. "Grizzly" could carry bombs, chemical tanks, napalm and even torpedoes. Only two XA-38 were built, Army s/n 314406 and 314407, with 314406 delivered to the Army at Wright Field on July 7, 1945. Both airplanes were scrapped after the war. Wingspan was 67.08 feet, length 51.7 feet. XA-38 illustrated shows gunner's control compartment aft, top turret and 75 mm nose cannon.

AT-10 utilized for flight tests of V-tail configuration in 1944-1945 at the Beech factory.

Closeup view of XA-38 engines and 75 mm nose-mounted cannon.

Instrument panel of 1961 Model 35-A33 Debonair, c/n CD-330, N252AA. Magneto switch is between throttle and propeller control.

MODEL 35-33 DEBONAIR

Beech developed the Debonair to compete primarily with the new, high performance airplanes like Piper's Commanche and Cessna's Model 182. Priced at $19,995 (standard airplane) the four-place Debonair was intended to be distinctly different than its cousin, the Model 35 Bonanza, yet retain traditional Beechcraft quality and performance. A conventional empennage assembly was used that immediately set the Debonair apart from the Model 35. First flown on September 14, 1959, the new Beechcraft featured a very spartan interior and only exterior trim paint. When introduced in November, 1959, initial interest was strong and 233 airplanes were built the first year. Dealer acceptance was good, but Beech salesmen soon found it hard to sell the Debonair against the competition, not because of price or quality but because the airplane's general appearance and interior appointments were too basic and utilitarian. Powered by a six-cylinder, fuel-injected 225 hp Continental IO-470-J engine swinging a two-blade, constant-speed Hartzell propeller, the Model 35-33 had a maximum speed of 195 mph at sea level and a gross weight of 2,900 pounds. Debonair illustrated is c/n CD-1, N831R, Model 33-35 prototype.

MODEL 35-B33 DEBONAIR

The Model 35-B33 was produced from late 1961 through 1964, and received further refinements found on the production Model 35 Bonanza. A new instrument panel was installed (same as P35 Bonanza), a small fairing added to the vertical stabilizer, the front seat backs were adjustable, a stall warning horn replaced the light used on previous models and the N35 Bonanza leading edge fuel tanks offered 80 gallon capacity as an option. Exterior paint scheme was more sophisticated and landing gear extension speed increased to 165 mph. A total of 426 35-B33 were built. 1961 priced was $21,975 but increased to $23,500 in February, 1963. Engine remained 225 hp IO-470-K. B33 N829B is illustrated. Note mannequin in full business suit seated behind pilot.

MODEL 35-A33 DEBONAIR

Beech revised the Debonair in 1961 to make it more appealing to potential customers. Overall exterior paint was made standard, interior features such as sun visors, seat padding, chart box and small hat shelf were added. A33 c/n started with CD-251 and 154 were built. CD-251 -CD-300 equipped with Continental 225 hp IO-470-J. CD-301 and after had IO-470-K of 225 hp. Gross weight was 3,000 pounds and maximum speed 195 mph. Price increased to $21,750. Debonair illustrated has optional heated pitot tube.

MODEL 35-C33 DEBONAIR

1965 Model 35-C33 incorporated changes that made it more like the Model 35 Bonanza. The dorsal fairing was extended forward, a larger, third cabin window was optional and the aft seats were mounted on individual tracks and featured adjustable backs. Four-color exterior paint scheme and the Bonanza's cabin assist step were also standard. Gross weight increased 50 pounds to 3,050. 305 35-C33 were produced from 1965-1967. Service ceiling was 17,800 feet, standard fuel capacity 50 gallons (80 gallons optional).

MODEL 35-C33A DEBONAIR

In 1966, Beech offered the 285 hp 35-C33A equipped with Continental IO-520-B engine. Distinguished from the C33 version by its exterior paint scheme, the C33A was developed to compete with Piper's 250 hp Commanche and to allow owners of older model Debonairs to step up in horsepower and performance. Maximum speed was 208 mph. A one-piece windshield improved overall appearance and became standard on all subsequent Debonair models. The engine installation was the same as the Model S35 Bonanza: canted down two degrees and right 2 1/2 degrees to reduce rudder force during takeoff and climb. Price was $29,875; later increased to $31,000.

MODEL D33 (EXPERIMENTAL)

In 1965, the U.S. Air Force experimented with a modified Model S35, c/n D-7859, N5847K, for possible application as a light, ground attack aircraft. A conventional tail was installed and the designation changed to Model D33. A variety of ordnance could be carried, including 250-pound napalm bombs, 272-pound general purpose (GP) bombs, 7.62 mm miniguns and 2.75-inch unguided rockets. Six wing hardpoints were provided, the inboard points stressed for 600 pounds and the outboard points stressed for 300 pounds. Tests were conducted at Eglin AFB, Florida. (Courtesy Larry A. Ball)

MODEL PD 249 (EXPERIMENTAL)

An improved version of c/n D-7859, PD 249 was evaluated by USAF for further investigations of the airplane's ground attack capabilities. A 350 hp Continental GIO-520 was installed for more power and a three-blade propeller was added. Wing hardpoints remained unchanged. Although tests were promising, the Air Force did not pursue extended development of the PD 249 and the project was cancelled in the early 1970s. PD 249 is illustrated with ordnance on all six wing hardpoints and overall three-tone camouflage scheme. (Courtesy Larry A. Ball).

MODEL E33 BONANZA

In the 1968 model year, the Debonair became a Bonanza in name only, although both models were very similar in appearance, appointments and performance. Equipped with a 225 hp Continental IO-470 engine, the E33 had a maximum speed of 195 mph at sea level, carried 50 gallons of fuel in standard tanks (80-gallon tanks optional), and had a sea level rate of climb of 930 feet per minute. Gross weight: 3,050 pounds. Useful load: 1,188 pounds. The third cabin window, optional on earlier Debonairs, was made standard on the E33. A total of 116 Model E33 Bonanzas were produced in 1968-1969 model years. Price: $31,750. Note the new, larger "Speed Sweep" windshield introduced by Beech on the 1968 Model 33 and 35 Bonanzas.

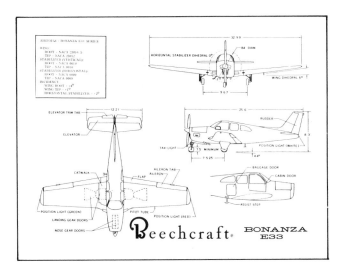

MODEL E33A BONANZA

Offered in the 1968-1969 model years, the Model E33A was identical to the E33 except for its 285 hp Continental IO-520-B powerplant. Maximum speed increased to 208 mph, sea level rate of climb was 1,200 feet per minute with a service ceiling of 18,300 feet. Beech included a Mark 12A nav/com radio as standard equipment, later changed to the solid-state Mark 16 unit. Price: $35,750. 79 E33A were produced in 1968-1969. (Courtesy Larry A. Ball)

MODEL E33B/E33C

Aerobatic versions of the E33 and E33A, the Model E33B and E33C were very similar except for customer choice of engines. The E33B had 225 hp, the E33C had 285 hp and became the preferred type; no E33B were produced. Both models were licensed in the acrobatic category at 2,800 pounds gross weight or could operate at their full 3,300-pound maximum gross weight in the utility category. Primary structural changes to the standard E33-series were Queen Air aileron ribs; horizontal stabilizer used Travel Air front and rear spars; heavier gauge skin thickness on vertical stabilizer leading edge; larger rudder cables and additional stringers in aft fuselage section. 25 Model E33C were built. Price: $38,250. During aerobatic flight, only the two front seats were occupied and a quick-release door was standard equipment, along with front seat shoulder harnesses, a g-meter and special fuel boost pump and unique checkerboard paint on wing and tail tips. Typical aerobatic maneuvers approved were aileron roll, barrel roll, inside loop, Immelman, Cuban eight and split-S. Two Model E33C are illustrated. (Courtesy Larry A. Ball)

MODEL F33 BONANZA

The 1970 Model F33 Bonanza was actually a refined Model E33, still using the Continental IO-470-K of 225 hp. F33 had restyled third cabin window of the Model V35B, "Speed Sweep" windshield, three gear down annunciator lights, redesigned subpanels and switches, a lower glareshield and Hartwell quick-opening latches for the engine cowling. Empty weight increased to 1,885 pounds, maximum gross weight was 3,050 pounds. Maximum speed remained at 195 mph. Priced at $34,150 each, 20 Model F33 were produced, all in the 1970 model year.

MODEL F33A BONANZA

Two different versions of the F33A were built, the short-fuselage model produced in 1970 and the long-fuselage model built in 1971, featuring a 19-inch extension in the aft cabin section. 26 F33A were built with short fuselages. 34 were produced with the long fuselage, allowing two important benefits: a larger baggage door and six-seat configuration previously available only in the Model V35B Bonanza. The 1971 F33A possessed all of the V35B's glamour, both inside and out, with the only difference between airplanes being the choice of empennage design. Maximum speed was 208 mph at sea level, but the higher gross weight of 3,400 pounds decreased rate of climb to 1,136 feet per minute and service ceiling to 17,500 feet. Price of the short-cabin F33A was $38,150 while the long-cabin version cost $41,600. 1983 Model F33A Bonanza is illustrated.

MODEL F33C BONANZA

Five F33C aerobatic Bonanzas were built in 1970 and all were short-fuselage airplanes. No F33C were built in 1971-1972. From 1973 on, all Model F33C Bonanzas featured the 19-inch longer fuselage and the same structural features of the earlier Model E33C aerobatic Bonanza. Powered by a 285 hp Continental IO-520-BB engine, the F33A seated four or five with optional fifth seat. Maximum gross weight: 3,400 pounds; useful load: 1,248 pounds. 23 F33C were built in 1986, including 21 for the Mexican Air Force: c/n CJ-156-CJ-176. Mexican Air Force F33C is illustrated, flown by Beech production flight test pilot Gale McKinney. Note vortex generators on wing leading edge. 1987 Model F33C cost $184,500 at the factory.

MODEL G33 BONANZA

Beech created the 1972 Model G33 Bonanza by taking the Model F33 and installing a 260 hp Continental IO-470-N powerplant. Only 50 G33 were built before production ended in 1973. Gross weight: 3,300 pounds. Price: $41,450. 1972 G33 had the improved interior configuration of the 1972 Model V35B Bonanza. Maximum speed: 204 mph. Range with 80 gallons of fuel (optional tanks): 1,243 statute miles. (Courtesy Larry A. Ball)

MODEL 34 TWIN-QUAD

The postwar feeder airline market look promising in 1945 and Beech Aircraft Corporation forged ahead with design of the Model 34 Twin-Quad, intended to fulfill the requirements of upstart and established feeder operators. The novel propulsion arrangement of two engines (with individual clutch assemblies) in each wing driving a single propeller through a common gearbox was designed by Beech engineer Alex Odevseff. Engineers W.A. Day, J.W. Massey and W.O. Stephens also contributed their talents to the Model 34 project. Featuring a large, V-tail empennage, the 20-passenger, high-wing Beechcraft made its first flight in October, 1947 from Beech Field. Powered by four, eight-cylinder Lycoming geared, supercharged, opposed GSO-580 engines developing 400 hp each at 3300 rpm,

the Twin-Quad could carry 1,000 pounds of express cargo and had a range of 1,400 statute miles with 45 minute fuel reserves while cruising at 180 mph. Although the airplane was designed for a maximum speed of 300 mph, that figure was never attained during the more than 200 hours of extensive flight testing accomplished from October, 1947 to January, 1949. Wingspan was 70 feet, length 53 feet and height to top of the V-tail nearly 18 feet. Maximum design gross weight was 20,000 pounds. Fuselage keel was designed to withstand gear-up landing loads and one unintentional landing incident demonstrated that the airplane could survive such an occurrence with minimal damage. The prototype (NX90521) made a forced landing on January 17, 1949 shortly after takeoff and was damaged beyond economical repair. (Refer to Appendix C, #8)

In-flight view of Model 34 Twin Quad over Wichita, Kansas.

1934 and present-day Beechcraft production facilities at left and right, surrounded by a montage of planes produced, are portrayed in this 1960's-vintage photo. ▼

Beech engineers, technicians and Walter H. Beech pose in front of the Model 34 Twin Quad engine test stand facility. Mr. Beech is sixth from left. The engines used to test the gearbox/clutch assemblies were surplus, 450 hp Lycoming units.

MODEL 35 BONANZA

A legend in its own right, the Beechcraft Model 35 Bonanza flew for the first time on December 22, 1945 with veteran Beech test pilot Vern L. Carstens at the wheel. The Bonanza met Walter H. Beech's demand for an airplane that would carry four people and their baggage in car-like comfort at 180 mph. Five engineers were assigned by Ted Wells to design the Model 35. Ralph Harmon led the team composed of Noel Naidenoff, Alex Odevseff, Jerry Gordon and Wilson Erhart (all but Erhart are known to have worked on the challenging XA-38 "Grizzly" project in 1944-1945). Certification was granted on March 25, 1947 and production of the first version, the Model 35, occurred in 1947-1948. 1,500 were built, more than any other Bonanza model. Powered by a 165 hp Continental E-165 opposed engine, the "straight 35" had a range of 750 statute miles on 40 gallons of fuel. Later production Model 35s had E-185-1 engines developing 185 hp for one minute at 2300 rpm, 165 hp continuous. Gross weight was 2,550 pounds. Price: $7,975 from c/n D-1 - c/n D-973, then increased to $8,945 from c/n D-974 - c/n D-1500. Model 35 illustrated was built in March, 1947. Famous V-tail was mounted at 30 degrees from horizontal. Tricycle gear was electrically operated and rugged enough for unimproved landing fields. The nose gear was not steerable on original Model 35 Bonanzas. Wood propeller featured controllable pitch but no governor device.

MODEL A35 BONANZA

Built in 1949, the Model A35 Bonanza was the first to incorporate a box-type, sheet metal spar carrythrough that replaced the tubular design used in the 1947-1948 airplanes and it was the first Bonanza to be licensed in the Utility category at full gross weight of 2,650 pounds. A total of 701 A35 were produced. Other changes were: gear down speed increased from 105 mph to 125 mph; flap extended speed increased to 105 mph; steerable nosewheel installation; useful load increased to 1,070 pounds. Model A35 illustrated has optional overall exterior paint scheme and was the 2,000th Model 35 built.

MODEL B35 BONANZA

The Model B35 Bonanza had all the improvements found in the A35 but featured the Continental E-185-8 engine that developed 196 hp for one minute at 2450 rpm. Priced at $11,975, 480 B35 were produced during the 1950 sales year. Flap extension increased from 20 to 30 degrees, front and rear cabin armrests and chart pockets were minor improvements found on the Model B35. B35 illustrated has standard exterior paint scheme. Note baggage door located on right side.

◄ MODEL 35 BONANZA "WAIKIKI BEECH"

Captain William Odom's famous record transoceanic flight was made in March, 1949 flying Beechcraft Model 35 Bonanza c/n D-4. Man and machine flew 4,957 miles nonstop from Hickam Field, Territory of Hawaii to Teterboro Airport in northern New Jersey. Flying time was 36 hours, 2 minutes. Odom is shown in this photograph with c/n D-4 after the historic flight.

1948 Model 35 Bonanza in optional overall paint scheme.

MODEL C35/D35/E35 BONANZA

The Model C35 Bonanza was built from late 1950 through the 1952 sales year. Significant changes included a more powerful Continental E-185-11 developing 185 hp continuous and 205 hp at takeoff for one minute. Chord of the V-tail was increased 20% and the V-angle increased to 33 degrees. Gross weight was 2,700 pounds and maximum speed 190 mph. 719 C35 were manufactured and were priced at $12,990 initially but increased to $18,990 in 1952. Model D35 of 1952 had new exterior paint scheme and 298 were produced. D35 sold for $18,990. 1954 Model E35 Bonanza offered two engines: E-185-11 of 185 hp continuous or the new Continental E-225-8 developing 225 hp at takeoff for one minute at 2450 rpm. Model E35 cost $18,990 with E-185-11, $19,990 with E-225-8 engine. 1951 Model C35 is illustrated. Note retracted assist step.

190 mph Model F35 Bonanza flies over Wichita, Kansas.

1948 Model 35 Bonanza instrument panel. Note color-coded arcs and radial lines on airspeed indicator required on all civil aircraft after 1946. Top of white arc for flap extension is 100 mph.

1950 Model C35 instrument panel shows refinement in instrument and control placement. Note flat, energy-absorbing control wheel first installed on Model B35 Bonanza.

MODEL F35 - MODEL M35 BONANZA

Beech added a third cabin window to the 1955 Model F35 Bonanza along with heavier aluminum skin thickness on the wing leading edges and strengthening of the V-tail spar cap. F35 was available with E-185-11 or E-225-8 engine and most customers preferred the higher horsepower E-225-8. 392 Model F35 were built and cost $19,990 with the 225 hp Continental. The 1956 Model G35 featured the E-225-8 as standard equipment, gross weight was 2,775 pounds gear extension speed increased to 140 mph. Windshield thickness increased to 1/4 inch. 476 G35 were produced. Price was $21,990. Model H35 of 1957 featured new 240 hp O-470-G engine, Model 50 Twin Bonanza wing spar caps and leading edge skin of reduced thickness and V-tail spar caps and elevators were strengthened. 464 Model H35 were manufactured, priced at $22,650 each. In 1958, the Model J35 was the first fuel-injected Bonanza, using Continental's 250 hp IO-470-C and cost $24,300. 396 Model J35 were built. The Model K35 Bonanza was first to have 50 gallon fuel capacity and optional fifth seat in aft cabin. Gross weight was 2,950 pounds. A total of 436 Model K35 were manufactured in the 1959 sales year. K35 cost $25,300. Maximum speed: 210 mph. There were no significant changes to the 1960 Model M35 Bonanza except for a new wingtip design. 400 M35 were produced. 1956 Model G35 is illustrated.

38

MODEL N35/P35 BONANZA

Beech revamped the already classic Bonanza in 1961 by adding a new, larger third cabin window and installing a 260 hp Continental IO-470-N engine in the Model N35. Gross weight increased to 3,125 pounds but the extra weight caused rate of climb to decrease from the Model M35's 1,170 fpm (feet per minute) to 1,150 fpm. 280 Model N35 Bonanzas were produced. Price was $26,500. The 1962

MODEL S35 BONANZA

Produced in the 1964-1965 model year, the Model S35 Bonanza's fuselage length was increased 19 inches allowing six occupants to be seated in the cabin when optional fifth/sixth seats were installed. The third cabin window was reshaped and Continental's IO-520-B engine brought 285 hp to the Bonanza for the first time. The fuel-injected powerplant was mounted in a redesigned cradle that was canted down 2 degrees and right 2 1/2 degrees to reduce rudder forces during takeoff and climb. The S35 Bonanza was also the fastest built up to that time, with a maximum speed of 212 mph. A total of 667 Model S35 were built. Price: $28,750.

1956 Model G35 Bonanza instrument panel shows padded glareshield and center-mounted engine instrument cluster.

Model P35 Bonanza had a completely redesigned instrument panel featuring avionics mounted to the right of center panel, new subpanels and all flight instruments were shock-mounted in a separate, hinged panel in front of the pilot. 467 Model P35 were built. Price: $27,650. Model N35 Bonanza illustrated shows fixed assist step first installed on Model N35.

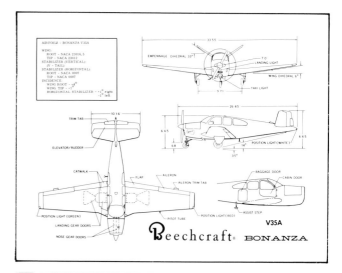

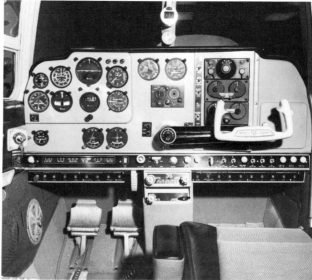

Model S35 Bonanza instrument panel illustrates new design first installed on the Model P35. Subpanels house switches, avionics are mounted within reach of either front seat occupant.

MODEL V35/V35A BONANZA

Beech introduced the Model V35 Bonanza in 1966, powered with the 285 hp Continental IO-520-B that gave a maximum speed of 210 mph at sea level. Gross weight was 3,400 pounds. There were few changes from the Model S35 Bonanza, the most salient being a one-piece windshield. Price was $32,500. 543 Model V35 Bonanzas were produced in 1966-1967. In 1968, the Model V35A featured the new "Speed-Sweep" windshield of increased area. The leading edge of the windshield was mounted six inches farther forward than previous Bonanzas and possessed 12 degrees more slope angle. A total of 426 Model V35A were built. In 1968 Beech renamed the Debonair "Bonanza" and all subsequent Model 35s were denoted by the prefix "V", with each derivative version identified by a suffix letter. The 1968 V35A was the first Bonanza to adopt the new classification system. Maximum speed: 210 mph; service ceiling: 17,500 feet. Price: $36,850. 1966 Model V35 Bonanza is illustrated. Note fixed assist step.

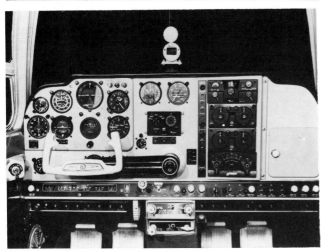

Beechcraft **BONANZA V35B**

MODEL V35TC/V35A-TC/V35B-TC BONANZA

Beech developed the turbocharged Model V35TC in 1966 when turbocharging and high altitude flying were becoming more commonplace for general aviation airplanes. Using the Continental 285 hp TSIO-520-D, the V35TC could maintain full rated power up to 19,000 feet where it had a maximum speed of 250 mph. Priced at $37,750, 79 V35TC were produced in 1966-1967. Oxygen system and electro-thermal propeller deice were two popular options for the Model V35TC Bonanza. For 1968-1969 model years, the Model V35A-TC incorporated the "Speed-Sweep" windshield and other improvements found on the naturally-aspirated Model V35A. A total of 46 Model V35A-TC were built. Price: $42,750. The last turbocharged Beechcraft Bonanza until the Model A36TC of 1979 was the 1970 Model V35B-TC. Only seven were produced. Three gear down annunciator lights were standard, Baron-type fuel gauges were installed and Hartwell quick-release cowling latches were employed. Powered by a 285 hp TSIO-520-D powerplant, The V35B-TC's maximum speed was 250 mph at 19,000 feet with a cruise speed of 230 mph at 24,000 feet, full throttle/2500 rpm. Model V35B-TC was not produced in 1971. 1966 Model V35TC Bonanza is illustrated.

1966 Model V35 Bonanza instrument panel.

MODEL V35B BONANZA

1970 was the first year for the Model V35B Bonanza. Only minor changes were implemented, including three gear down annunciator lights, anti-slosh fuel bladder cells and new interior styling. 218 V35B were produced in 1970. Price: $41,600. The 1972 Model V35B received a major interior redesign that required structural changes to the upper cabin sections. More durable materials were employed and the overhead fresh air ventilation system was improved. Price was $41,600 and 104 were built in 1972. In 1978 the V35B received a 24-volt electrical system, 4-second gear retraction/extension time. Beech built the 10,000th Model 35

Bonanza, c/n D-10000, on February 9, 1977. The airplane was flown on a nationwide tour to celebrate the Model 35's 30-year dominance of the high performance, single-engine market. The last Model 35 built was V35B c/n D-10403, delivered to Beech production flight test department on November 11, 1982 and delivered to a Beech dealer in May, 1984. Last Model 35 delivered to a retail customer was V35B c/n D-10399, delivered in August, 1984. Model V35B N35YR, painted to celebtrate 35 years of Bonanza production in 1982, is illustrated flown by Beech production test pilot Bob Buettgenbach.

MODEL O35 BONANZA (EXPERIMENTAL)

Beech built the Model O35 Bonanza in 1961 as an experimental testbed featuring a laminar flow wing with integral (wet) fuel cells in the leading edge, replacing rubber bladder tanks. The tricycle landing gear was modified with trailing beam-type main gear assemblies and new gear doors. The nose gear remained unchanged. A 260 hp Continental IO-470-N engine powered the O35. Despite the advantage of increased fuel capacity, wingtip fuel filler access and smoother landing gear operation, the O35 was not developed beyond the experimental stage. (Courtesy Larry A. Ball)

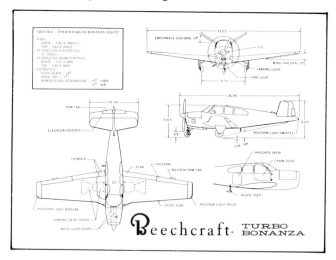

Model V35B instrument panel with engine instrument cluster at center, flight instruments on shock-mounted panel, subpanel switches/autopilot mode controller at left and circuit breakers on right subpanel.

MODEL 36/A36 BONANZA

Based on the 1968 Model E33 Bonanza, Beech's Model 36 was created by moving the E33A's aft cabin bulkhead back 19 inches and adding a 10-inch section to the fuselage. The wing was relocated aft, placing pilot and passengers 10 inches farther forward on the wing, thereby increasing the CG range and stability of the airplane. Two outward-opening doors were installed on the right fuselage side that permitted easy passenger or cargo loading and unloading. The doors could be removed for flight. Powered by a 285 hp Continental IO-520 engine, maximum speed was 204 mph and the Model 36 was licensed in the Utility category at its maximum gross weight of 3,600 pounds. An immediate success when introduced in June, 1968, the Model 36 was primarily aimed at the air taxi or light cargo market. Three interiors were offered: standard, utility and a deluxe design. Priced at $40,650, 105 were built in 1968 and 79 in 1969. In 1970 Beech added a more luxurious interior similar to the Model V35B, three gear down annunciator lights, Hartwell quick-release cowling latches and redesigned instrument subpanels to create the Model A36 Bonanza. Redesigned wing tips

changed span from 32 feet 10 inches on the Model 36 to 33 feet six inches on the A36. 56 were built in 1970 and 42 in 1971. In 1972 electrically-operated, vertical-readout engine instruments were standard and in 1978 a 24-volt electrical system and 4-second gear retraction/extension time were incorporated, beginning with A36 c/n E-1111. A major change occurred in 1984 when Beech completely redesigned the instrument panel. Separate shaft-type control wheels, circular, vertically-stacked engine instruments were mounted on the new instrument panel that was canted back at the top for easier pilot scanning, and quadrant-mounted throttle/propeller/mixture controls were installed. Small, wedge-like vortex generators were added to the outboard wing leading edge for improved roll control at high angle of attack. The engine changed to a 300 hp (takeoff and continuous) Continental IO-550-B. Takeoff gross weight increased to 3,650 pounds. 95 A36 were built in 1984. A36 illustrated is flown by Beech production test pilot (and three-time women's national aerobatic champion) Joyce Case.

MODEL A36TC BONANZA

After a nine-year absence, Beech reentered the single-engine turbocharged market in 1979 with the Model A36TC Bonanza powered by a Continental TSIO-520-UB engine developing 300 hp. Beech engineers eliminated cowl flaps by designing a series of air cooling louvers that provided adequate airflow inside the engine

compartment. The absence of cowl flaps was viewed as both a reduction in maintenance and pilot workload. The standard Model A36 Bonanza cabin heating system was revised to produce 20% more heat to keep cabin occupants warm during high altitude flights. The A36TC was a welcome addition to Beech's product line and 32 were produced the first year, from c/n EA-1 to c/n EA-32. Fuel capacity remained at 74 gallons useable and maximum certificated altitude was 25,000 feet. A36TC illustrated is c/n EA-1, N36TC, a company demonstrator.

MODEL B36TC BONANZA

Sales success with the Model A36TC led to the improved Model B36TC in 1981. Significant changes were incorporated into the turbocharged, six-seat Beechcraft, including a completely redesigned instrument panel with separate, shaft-type control wheels, quadrant-mounted throttle/propeller/mixture controls and circular, vertically-mounted engine instruments. Fuel capacity was increased to 108 gallons maximum (102 gallons useable) and wingspan increased from 33 feet, 6 inches (A36TC) to 37 feet, 10 inches. Wedge-like, vortex generators were installed on the wing leading edge to improve roll control at high angle of attack. Minor improvements were made to the engine/turbocharger installation and air conditioning was available as an option. Maximum takeoff gross weight increased to 3,850 pounds. Engine: Continental TSIO-520-UB rated at 300 hp (continuous). Cruise speed at maximum power (31 inches Hg manifold pressure/2400 rpm): 200 knots TAS (true airspeed), ISA conditions at 25,000 feet. B36TC c/n start at EA-242 and 50 were built in 1982, 65 in 1983. 1987 c/n start with EA-462.

MODEL T36TC (EXPERIMENTAL)

Beech engineers modified a basic Model A36 Bonanza fuselage with newly-designed T-tail for experimental flight testing intended to investigate the feasability of a pressurized, single-engine Bonanza. Designated c/n EC-1 (N2065T) the T36TC was an unpressurized testbed powered by a 325 hp Continental TSIO-520 engine with aft-mounted turbocharger, requiring a 12-inch extension forward of the windshield to accomodate the powerplant. The T36TC made its first flight on February 16, 1979 with Beech engineering test pilots Lou Johansen and Robert Suter at the controls. A total of 82 hours, 45 minutes of testing were accumulated during 89 flights, with the last flight made on January 25, 1980. T36TC illustrated flown by Lou Johansen. ▼

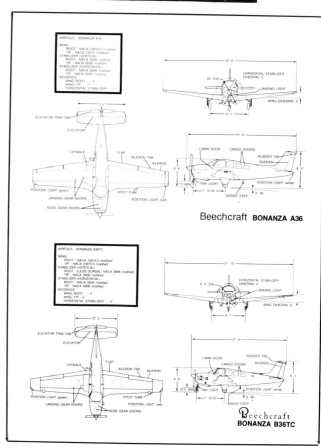

MODEL 1079 (MILITARY)

Built for the U.S. Air Force to perform electronic surveillance missions during the conflict in Southeast Asia, the Model 1079 was designated "Pave Eagle II" and were improved versions of the Model 1074 "Pave Eagle I" (highly modified Model E33A). Also known as QU-22B, the Model 1079 were Model A36 Bonanzas equipped with tip tanks for increased fuel capacity and endurance on station, 375 hp Continental engines with special reduction gearboxes to turn the propeller at a very low rpm for noise reduction. QU-22B was designed to be flown by remote control on missions with a pilot and observer on board to monitor equipment, but could also be hand-flown by the pilot if necessary. Note tip tanks and aft two cabin windows that are blanked out.

MODEL 45 MENTOR

First flown on December 2, 1948 by Beech test pilot Vern L. Carstens, the Model 45 Mentor originated as a private venture by Beech Aircraft Corporation to develop a basic trainer for military service. Featuring a full-vision, three-segment canopy over the two cockpits, the Mentor was based primarily on the commercial Model 35 Bonanza. Major departures from the Model 35 were a conventional empennage (Beech did consider a V-tail for the Model 45) and narrow fuselage. The prototype was powered by a Continental E-185 engine rated at 185 hp (takeoff), 165 hp continuous and had a maximum speed of 176 mph and a cruise speed of 160 mph at 10,000 feet. Gross weight was 2,650 pounds. Stressed for 10 positive and 4.5 negative G, the Mentor was tough and could perform all aerobatic maneuvers taught by most military services around the world. Model 45 illustrated is early prototype. Note general similarity to Model 35. ▼

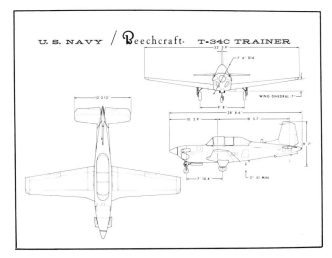

MODEL 45 - T-34A

The U.S. Air Force ordered three YT-34 in 1950 for service evaluation as a basic trainer. Satisfied with every aspect of the rough-and-ready Mentor, the air force ordered an initial production batch in 1953, designated T-34A. Two were delivered in September, 1953 and 88 were delivered by September, 1954. A total of 353 T-34A were built before production ended in October, 1956. The USAF received another 100 T-34A and the Royal Canadian Air Force (RCAF) took delivery of 25 Mentors built by the Canadian Car and Foundry Co., Ltd of Fort William, Ontario after obtaining a manufacturing license from Beech in 1954. YT-34 was powered by a 220 hp Continental E-225-8 engine and had a maximum speed of 188 mph, cruised at 173 mph with a service ceiling of 20,000 feet. Gross weight was 2,950 pounds. USAF T-34A featured Continental O-470-13 engine rated at 225 hp giving a maximum speed of 189 mph. Gross weight was 2,950 pounds. YT-34 is illustrated during USAF evaluation.

MODEL 45 - T-34B

The U.S. Navy also purchased the Beechcraft Mentor for use as its primary trainer. After exhaustive operational evaluation the Navy started taking delivery of the T-34B in December, 1954. A total of 423 T-34B were produced for the U.S. Navy between October, 1954 and October, 1957 when the last 12 airplanes were delivered. Powered by a Continental O-470-13 engine developing 225 hp, the T-34B had a maximum speed of 188 mph and gross weight of 2,985 pounds. The Navy continued using the T-34B until the late 1970s when the turbine-powered Beech Model T-34C began to replace the aging trainers. Beech granted Model B45 Mentor (export version) production licenses to Japan in 1953 and Argentina in 1956. Fuji Heavy Industries built 137 for Japan's Air Self Defense Force (JASDF) and another 36 for the Philippine Air Force. Argentina assembled 75 Mentors in Cordoba for military service. Beech exported 318 Model B45. Total number of T-34's built between 1948-1958: 1,904. U.S. Navy T-34B is illustrated. ▼

Model 45 Mentor as T-34B for U.S. Navy evaluation. Note exhaust augmentor tubes.

MODEL T-34C/T-34C-1 TURBINE MENTOR

In 1972-1973, Beech reengineered the venerable Model T-34, transforming it into a powerful, economical and rugged turboprop trainer designated Model T-34C and Model T-34C-1. The U.S. Navy evaluated the T-34C version, powered by a Pratt & Whitney PT6A-25 engine of 400 shp (shaft horsepower) in 1973, and purchased 18 in 1975, to be followed over the next seven years by over 330 T-34C trainers. The Model T-34C-1, powered by a 550 shp version of Pratt & Whitney's PT6A-25 turboprop engine, was designed as an export trainer with light ground attack capabilities. Initial deliveries began in 1977 when the Ecuadorian Air Force accepted six of 14 T-34C-1. Peru, Morocco, Argentina and Indonesia also ordered Beechcraft Model T-34C-1 for their military services. Trio of T-34C-1 illustrated were delivered to Peru, Morocco and Ecuador. (Refer to T-44A for T-34C photograph) The U.S. Navy took delivery of an additional 19 T-34C in 1989-1990.

1946 Beechcraft "Plainsman" automobile, built in mockup form only, featured air-cooled aircraft engine for power, electric drive for wheels, automatic air suspension, six-seat capacity. 2,200-pound car capitalized on aerodynamics for 25 mpg economy.

Fastback design and Bonanza-type doors that curved into roof, generous window area were salient features of Beech Plainsman. Crash protection was integral part of design. Anticipated selling price was about $5,000.

MODEL 50 TWIN BONANZA

Designed as a light, multi-engine airplane marketed between the Model 35 Bonanza and the larger, heavier Beechcraft Model D18S, the Model 50 Twin Bonanza went from drawing board to first flight in only 223 days, taking off from Beech Field on November 11, 1949 for its maiden flight under the able command of Vern Carstens. The Twin Bonanza shared many parts with the single-engine Model 35 Bonanza, and was an obvious step-up airplane for the Model 35 owner. Development and accelerated testing continued through 1950 and CAA certification was granted in May, 1951. Only three Model 50 were delivered in 1951. Two Lycoming GO-435-C2 engines rated at 260 hp turned two-blade, constant-speed, full-feathering propellers. The Twin Bonanza could carry three abreast in the front seats and two in the aft cabin section. Gross weight was 5,500 pounds. Beech's Model 50 was one of the first light twins after the war to gain acceptance by businessmen, and helped pave the way for later developments like the Model 65 Queen Air. Model 50 Twin Bonanza illustrated has taxi light in nose cap, exhaust augmentor tubes and retractable assist step. Model 35 Bonanza influence is apparent, especially in cabin area.

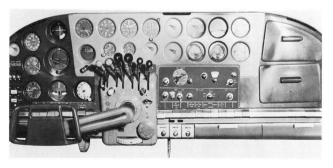

Model 50 Twin Bonanza instrument panel grouped all flight instruments in front of the pilot, placed engine controls to left of center for comfort of middle seat occupant.

YL-23-L-23A SEMINOLE

In 1951, the United States Army Field Forces Board evaluated the Beechcraft Model 50 Twin Bonanza at Fort Bragg, North Carolina and ordered four as general and staff personnel transports. Designated YL-23, the four ships were delivered in early 1952 and 60 airplanes were ordered to meet the Army's needs in the Korean Conflict, virtually dominating Beech's entire Twin Bonanza production for 1952-1953. The first L-23A was delivered in February, 1953 and 55 were in the hands of the Army by September. Engines: Lycoming GO-435-C2 rated at 260 hp. Maximum speed: 202.5 mph. Range: 1,155 statute miles. In 1957, the U.S. Army returned aging L-23A and L-23B for a complete rebuild into L-23D configuration, with six seats, 340 hp engines and 7,000 pound gross takeoff weight. The first U.S. Army YL-23 is illustrated.

L-23B/U-8D SEMINOLE

The L-23B version of the Model B50 began delivery to the U.S. Army Field Forces in September, 1953, when five airplanes were accepted. L-23B was equivalent to the Model B50 Twin Bonanza that entered commercial production in December, 1953 for the 1954 model year. Beech had incorporated over 100 improvements to the Model 50 from 1951-1953 during manufacture of the Army YL-23 and L-23A airplanes. Like the B50, the L-23B benefitted from lessons learned in military service; gross weight was up to 6,000 pounds, maximum speed was 205 mph and seating for six was standard. A total of 40 L-23B were delivered to the Army by April, 1954 when production terminated. In 1958, many L-23B were returned to Beech for a complete rebuilding into L-23D configuration, equivalent to the commercial Model F50 Twin Bonanza powered by 340 hp Lycoming GSO-480-B1B6 engines. L-23B illustrated displays overall olive drab paint except for anti-glare panels on nose and inboard nacelle sections. (Refer to Appendix C, #9)

U.S. Army L-23D/RU-8D with SLAR radar installation. Commercial equivalent was Model E50.

U.S. Army L-23E/U-8D personnel transport at Beech Field, 1956.

L-23D/U-8D SEMINOLE

First deliveries of the L-23D came in January, 1957 and were equivalent to the commercial Model E50 Twin Bonanza with 340 hp supercharged Lycoming GSO-480-A1A6 engines. Performance was essentially the same as Model E50. L-23D illustrated is equipped with "Project Michigan" AN/UPD-1 airborne radar.

L-23D SEMINOLE (SLAR)

In 1959, the U.S. Army equipped some Beechcraft L-23D models with the advanced APS 85 "SLAR" -side-looking airborne radar - designed to provide all-weather surveillance of the battleground/combat arena for intelligence purposes. ▼

48

MODEL B50 - J50 TWIN BONANZA

The Model 50 continued to mature from 1951-1963 when production stopped with the Model J50. First major improvements occurred in the 1953 Model B50 when gross weight, payload and speed all increased. In 1955, the Model C50 was introduced to answer the challenge presented by the Aero Commander 560, the Twin Bonanza's chief competitor. New, 275 hp Lycoming GO-480-F6 engines were installed that increased maximum speed to 210 mph with a cruise speed at 66% power of 200 mph at full gross weight. One C50 was built for the U.S. Army (c/n CH-123) as XL-23C/U-8G. 216 Model C50 were produced in 1955. The D50 series of the Twin Bonanza was most numerous model, with a total of 347 manufactured from 1956 to 1963 in five versions: D50, D50A, D50B, D50C and D50E. Minor airframe and systems changes denoted the different models. Built concurrently with the C50, the D50 featured 295 hp Lycoming GO-480-G2F6 swinging new, three-blade Hartzell propellers. Useful load increased to 2,319 pounds and range was 1,650 statute miles at a cruising speed of 203 mph. The Model E50 of 1957 featured 340 hp Lycoming GSO-480-A1A6 supercharged powerplants and the 1958 Model F50

mounted Lycoming GSO-480-B1B6 engines of 340 hp. 70 E50 and 25 F50 Twin Bonanzas were built. Produced in 1959, the Model G50 and the 1960 Model H50 also used Lycoming GSO-480-B1B6 but offered optional fuel injection with the IGSO-480-B1B6. Both models were faster, carried more fuel and payload than earlier airplanes. Last variant of the popular Twin Bonanza was the 1961 Model J50, with a more pointed, longer nose section, 340 hp Lycoming IGSO-480-A1B6 powerplants and seating for up to six occupants in its slightly enlarged cabin. Maximum speed reached 235 mph. Both the Model H50 and J50 featured airstair doors and redesigned, square wingtips. All Model 50s could be equipped with Aerojet-General JATO bottles at the factory if desired. Installed in the aft section of each nacelle, the bottles could be fired in case of engine failure after takeoff to boost airspeed to a safe level or used to augment takeoff power. A total of 24 G50, 30 H50 and 27 J50 Twin Bonanzas were produced. 883 Model 50 of all types were built between 1950-1963. Model H50 is illustrated. Note enlarged cabin window size. Third cabin window was standard on Model D50 and subsequent versions. Square wingtips were designed to improve single-engine climb rate.

MODEL 95-55 BARON

1961 saw the introduction of yet another light, multi-engine Beechcraft, joining the already successful Model 50 Twin Bonanza and its smaller counterpart the Model 95 Travel Air. Given the royal name Baron, the Model 95-55 was a slightly larger, more modern version of the Travel Air twin. Seating 4-5 people in its roomy cabin, the Baron was aimed at the businessman who wanted fast, economical aerial transportation. First flown February 29, 1960, the Model 95-55 housed its 260 hp Continental IO-470-L engines in compact, low-drag, flat nacelles and featured a swept tail with long dorsal fairing. Maximum speed was 236 mph with a range of 1,200 statute miles and 45-minute fuel reserve. The tricycle landing gear was electrically operated with a manual crank-down alternate extension system. Cabin heating was accomplished by a 50,000 BTU combustion-type heater using fuel from the left main tank when operating. Enthusiastically accepted by Beech dealers and pilots alike, 190 Barons were produced in 1961 and the future looked very bright for the new Beechcraft twin. Model 95-55 illustrated is an early production 1961 airplane.

MODEL A55 - B55 BARON

The Model 95-A55 was offered in the 1962 model year with optional six-seat interior, a gear extension speed of 175 mph with flaps extended to 15 degrees. Gross weight was 4,880 pounds. 187 Model 95-A55 were built in 1962 and 122 in 1963. In 1963, Beech built 19 Model A55 airframes (no engines) and shipped them to France to be used by its European affiliate SFERMA (Societe Francaise d'Entretien et de Reparation de Materiel Aeronautique), with whom Beech had signed a technical aggreement for cooperative development of turboprop engines in Baron, Model 95 and Model 18 airplanes. Airframes were modified in France and fitted with two 450 shp Astazou IIJ turboprop engines, marketed under the name "Marquis" and produced by SFERMA. In America, the Baron had captured much of the light twin-engine market by 1964 when Beech introduced the improved Model 95-B55 to its product line. Primary changes were a 120-pound increase in gross weight to 5,000 pounds, a longer nose section that increased baggage space 50% or permitted installation of more remote avionics equipment. New Beechcraft two-blade, constant-speed, full-feathering propellers

were fitted to the B55 Baron and increased climb rate to 1,730 feet per minute with single-engine ceiling up to 7,770 feet at 5,000 pound gross weight. With the optional 140-gallon fuel tanks, the B55 Baron had a range of 1,225 statute miles at 10,000 feet altitude and 45% power setting. 114-gallon fuel tanks were standard. Lycoming IO-470-L engines of 260 hp were installed in the Model 95-B55 Baron. 271 were manufactured in 1964. Model B55 became mainstay of the Baron series from 1970 to 1982 when production stopped after 1,851 had been built (not including T-42A production of 70 airplanes). The B55 was an ideal entry-level multi-engine aircraft for the private or business pilot and its 260 hp engines provided both good performance and fuel economy. By 1971 the B55 had earned a solid reputation as an excellent light, twin-engine airplane and was becoming widely recognized for its inherent values of Beechcraft dependability and performance. Cruising speed was 225 mph at 7,000 feet, maximum speed 236 mph and a range of 1,225 statute miles could be achieved with optional 142-gallon fuel tanks. 1964 Model 95-B55 Baron is illustrated.

MODEL 95-B55 BARON - T-42A COCHISE

Beech received an order for the Model 95-B55 Baron in February, 1965 to serve the U.S. Army as instrument and multi-engine training aircraft. Dubbed T-42 and T-42A "Cochise", the company eventually built 65 Barons for the Army. The first five were delivered September 2, 1965 with olive drab and white exterior paint schemes. Later T-42A were painted overall olive drab. In 1971, Beech delivered five T-42A to the U.S. Army for use by the Turkish Army under the Military Assistance Program (MAP). Seven T-42A were sold to the the Spanish Air Force in 1972. Performance was essentially identical to Model 95-B55 Baron. T-42A is illustrated on a Beech test flight in U.S. Army livery.

MODEL 95-C55 - D55 BARON

Beech continued to improve the popular Baron series with introduction in 1966 of the Model 95-C55 Baron. Boasting more power than its predecessors, the C-55 featured 285 hp Continental IO-520-C powerplants, a one-piece windshield and minor refinement to the interior/exterior details of the airplane. 265 Model 95-C55 were produced in 1966 and the C55 was built concurrently with the Model 95-B55 Baron in 1967, with 185 C55 built. Production ended in 1967. The College of Air Training located in Hamble, England purchased 12 Model 95-C55 Barons in 1967 for use as trainers for British airline companies. Beech offered the Model D55 Baron in 1968 and 1969, with the Model 95-C55's IO-520 powerplants and the C55's larger horizontal stabilizer/elevator that spanned 15 feet 11 1/4 inches. 181 were built in 1968 and 135 in 1969 before production changed to the improved Model E55 Baron in 1970. Model D55 Baron is illustrated.

MODEL E55 BARON

First introduced in the 1970 model year, the Model E55 Baron was fitted with two Continental IO-520-C engines developing 285 hp and optional six-place seating not available on B/C/D55. Offered as an alternative airplane to the lower-powered Model 95-B55 Baron for those customers who demanded higher horsepower and more room, the E55's larger cabin could be equipped to accomodate six occupants or arranged for transport of light cargo with four seats removed. Maximum cruising speed was 230 mph and rate of climb 1,670 feet per minute. 59 were built in 1970 and production continued concurrently with the Model 95-B55 Baron until 1982 when manufacture of both models terminated. Although the E55 Baron did not sell in quantities like the B55, a total of 434 were produced from 1970-1982.

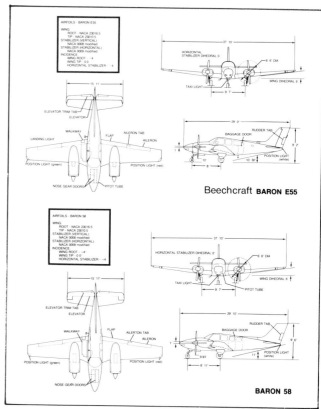

Beechcraft **BARON E55**

BARON 58

MODEL 56TC TURBO BARON

Using the Model 95-C55 Baron as a foundation for development, Beech engineered the powerful Model 56TC in 1965-1966 and the first example, c/n TG-1, was flown on May 25, 1966 by engineering test pilot Bob Hagan. Two Lycoming turbocharged, fuel-injected TIO-541-E1B4 engines, developing 380 hp at 2900 rpm/41.5 in. Hg manifold pressure, were housed in large cowlings with nacelles that swept back to the wing trailing edge. Wingspan was 37 feet, 10 inches and held 182 gallons of fuel in rubber bladder-type cells. Gross weight was 5,990 pounds. The 56TC featured six seats, two-engine rate of climb was 2,020 feet per minute and single-engine rate of climb was 412 feet per minute. Complete wing/tail surface and propeller deicing equipment was optional and virtually necessary to take full advantage of the high-flying 56TC's performance. Maximum allowable airspeed at 20,000 feet was 262 mph but the 56TC could achieve 300 mph TAS at 24,000 feet and full throttle, making it one of the fastest piston-powered light, multi-engine airplanes in the world in 1967. 82 Model 56TC Turbo Barons were produced from 1967-1969 when the improved Model A56TC was introduced. 1967 Model 56TC is illustrated equipped with wing/tail deice boots. 56TC had wing-mounted pitot tube.

MODEL A56TC TURBO BARON

Produced in 1970-1971, the Model A56TC Turbo Baron featured the same Lycoming engines as the 56TC but had increased fuel capacity of 207 gallons. Like the 56TC, the A56TC could carry 300 pounds of baggage in the nose compartment or accomodate remote-mounted avionics. Gross weight remained at 5,990 pounds.

Turbochargers were fully automatic and required no pilot workload. Single-engine service ceiling was 18,600 feet at gross weight, increasing to 23,000 feet at 5,000 pound gross weight. Only external change made to the A56TC was nose-mounted pitot tube and new paint scheme. Eleven Model A56TC Turbo Barons were built, c/n TG-84 through TG-94. The 56TC and A56TC were very similar in wing fuel system and powerplant installation to the 1966 Beechcraft Model 60 Duke prototype.

MODEL 58 BARON

In 1969, Beech took the six-seat fuselage/cabin design of the highly successful Model 36 Bonanza and mated it with the equally successful Model E55 Baron to create the versatile Model 58 Baron. First flown on June 23, 1969, the Baron 58 offered customers twin-engine performance and a spacious cabin that could be easily loaded and unloaded through double doors installed on the right side of the fuselage. Club seating, with the center two seats facing aft and the aft two seats facing forward, was a popular arrangement that permitted business meetings to take place while airborne, demonstrating just one of the Baron 58's many talents. Powered by two Continental IO-520-C engines rated at 285 hp, cruising speed was 230 mph at 7,000 feet with a maximum speed of 242 mph. Gross weight was 5,400 pounds. 98 were built in 1970 and Beech continued to improve the Model 58 through the 1986 version. Over 1,400 Model 58 Barons had been built by 1986. Wing/tail surface and electro-thermal propeller deice equipment was optional along with air conditioning.

MODEL 58TC BARON

First flight of the turbocharged, six-seat Beechcraft Model 58TC occurred on October 31, 1975. 310 hp TSIO-520 Continental engines were installed for optimum performance at high altitudes, fuel management was simplified in the 1976 58TC and wet cell fuel tanks were optional for the first time. Shoulder harnesses became standard equipment on all forward-facing seats and the flap system was revised with a three-position, pre-select type control switch (all Baron models had these improvements). A 1977 Model 58TC became the 40,000th Beechcraft built since the Model 17R of 1932. Major change for the 58TC came in 1978 when 325 hp Continental TSIO-520 powerplants replaced the 310 hp units. In production from 1976 to 1984, a total of 151 58TC were built. 1983 Baron 58TC is illustrated.

MODEL 58P BARON

Developed as a top-of-the-line Baron, the pressurized Model 58P set new standards of comfort and performance when introduced in 1974. First flown on August 16, 1973, the 58P had its double doors located on the left side of the fuselage, opposite that of the Model 58TC Baron. Pilot's entry door remained on the right side over the wing. Six seats were standard, arranged facing forward or the two center seats could be installed facing aft in the popular club arrangement. Baggage access was through the left side double doors. Using air from the two 310 hp Continental TSIO-520-LB1C engine's turbosuperchargers to pressurize the cabin, both pilot and passengers could experience the benefits of high altitude flying without the burden of wearing oxygen masks. Pressurization control was fully automatic once set by the pilot. A pressure differential of 3.6 psi kept the 58P's cabin at sea level when flying at 7,800 feet. At 18,000 feet airplane altitude the cabin was maintained at 7,800 feet. The pressurized Baron was assembled at Beech's Salina, Kansas facility and first deliveries began in 1976 when 83 were produced. Changes for the 1977 58P included shoulder harnesses for the front seats, easier fuel tank selection to reduce pilot workload, a three-position flap pre-select control switch and a wide choice of custom-installed avionics. Polyurethane exterior paint became standard on the 58P and all Baron models in 1978 and the pressurized Baron mounted new engines; 325 hp Continental TSIO-520-WB that increased cruising speed to 277 mph while maximum speed approached the magic 300 mph mark. Improved pressurization differential provided a sea level cabin up to 8,350 feet or a cabin altitude of 9,200 feet at 21,000 feet airplane altitude. Model 58P illustrated shows left-side double doors. (Refer to Appendix C, #10)

1984 Model 58P pressurized Baron instrument panel displays major change from earlier design. All engine instruments are circular, arranged in vertical stack. Panel is canted for easier viewing and subpanel switches are located for minimum pilot workload. Padded glareshield houses annunciator lights that monitor primary systems' status. ▼

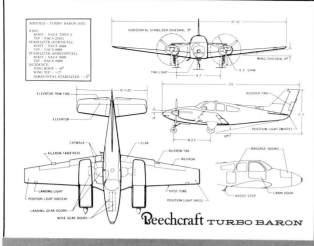

Beechcraft TURBO BARON

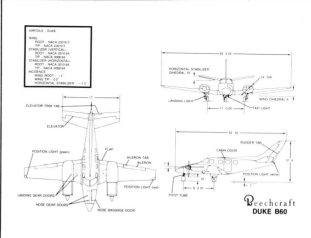

Beechcraft DUKE B60

MODEL 60 DUKE

Combining speed, superb comfort and very distinctive looks, the Beechcraft Model 60 Duke (c/n P-1) took to the air for the first time on December 29, 1966 under command of Beech test pilot Bob Hagan. The Duke's muscle came from two Lycoming TIO-541-E1A4 powerplants swinging three-blade, constant-speed, full-feathering propellers. Using air from the engine's turbosuperchargers, the cabin could be pressurized to 4.6 psid, providing sea level conditions up to 10,000 feet and a 10,000-foot

cabin altitude at 24,800 feet. Standard fuel capacity was 118 gallons but 170 gallons was available…a popular option with many Duke owners. Standard cabin configuration was four seats, with six seats optional. Maximum cruising speed was 278 mph at 25,000 feet and service ceiling was 30,800 feet. With 170-gallon tanks, the Duke could fly 973 statute miles at 271 mph at 25,000 feet. Maximum takeoff gross weight: 6,775 pounds. A total of 122 Model 60 were built from 1968-1970.

MODEL A60/B60 DUKE

Beech began delivering the improved Model A60 Duke in the latter half of 1970, when it replaced the Model 60 on the production line. The turbosuperchargers weighed less and featured internal changes that extended the life of this important engine component and permitted the TSIO-540-E1C4 engines to achieve full rated horsepower to a higher altitude. Maximum speed was 286 mph at 23,000 feet and service ceiling went up to 35,800 feet with the improved turbosuperchargers accounting for a large part of the Duke's enhanced performance. Fuel economy and cooler turbosupercharger operating temperatures were spinoff benefits that served to increase powerplant longevity. New interior fabrics and leathers were offered and the pressurization control system was revised to permit smoother overall operation and cabin comfort.

Model 60 illustrated exemplifies the Duke's sleek lines and one-of-a-kind appearance. With Duke sales running strong, Beech offered the Model B60 Duke in 1974 that featured a wider, longer cabin with redesigned seats for more passenger comfort. In 1975, the Duke received a redesigned, lightweight AiResearch pressurization system with Lexan valves and a mini-sized controller unit to save panel space. 1976 Duke owners could order new, wet-cell wingtip fuel tanks that held 30 gallons, increasing the B60's range to 1,287 statute miles at 65% power setting. TBO (time between overhaul) of the Duke's 380 hp TSIO-540-series engines increased to 1600 hours in 1977 and cruise speed went up again to 283 mph. After building 471 Model A60 and B60 Dukes, production ended in 1982 with B60 c/n P-596. Model A60 Duke is illustrated.

L-23F

Beech Aircraft Corporation's highly successful Model 50 series Twin Bonanza had served the U.S. Army since 1951, proving its worth as a military transport and electronic surveillance aircraft around the world. In 1958, the Army wanted a follow-on design and Beech modified the basic Model 50 by enlarging the cabin height, width and length, completely redesigning the interior to be easily adaptable to multi-mission tasks and adding three large cabin windows. The redesigned airplane was designated L-23F with a gross weight of 7,368 pounds. Ten seats could be installed in a high density configuration or the cabin would accomodate seven combat-ready troops with equipment. With seats removed, 1,350 pounds

of cargo could be loaded. Powered by two Lycoming IGSO-480-A1A6, -A1B6 or -A1E6 engines developing 340 hp, the L-23F had a maximum cruising speed of 214 mph and could climb to 27,000 feet. A total of 71 were delivered to the U.S. Army from 1960 to 1963. Some of the L-23Fs Beech built were modified into RL-23F configuration designed to mount battlefield surveillance radar systems for collection of combat intelligence information. Wingspan: 45 feet 10 1/2 inches. Gross weight later increased from 7,368 to 7,700 pounds. Range: 1,445 statute miles. Designation later changed from L-23F to U-8F. L-23F is illustrated in standard U.S. Army livery, May, 1960. (Refer to Appendix C, #11)

◄

Cockpit view of U.S. Army L-23F/U-8F "Seminole" utility transport. Quadrant has only throttle and propeller controls; mixture control was automatic on IGSO-540 engines. Manual enrichment capability was provided by two small levers forward of throttles. Gear handle is right of quadrant, flap control left of quadrant.

MODEL 65 QUEEN AIR

In 1958, Beech modified the L-23F into a commercial design known as the Model 65 Queen Air, the first Beechcraft to bear a royal designation. First flight was made on August 28, 1958. The Queen Air was a heavy piston-twin with a maximum gross weight of 7,700 pounds, room for six to eight cabin occupants plus a crew of two that were separated from the cabin by sliding doors. Two Lycoming IGSO-480-A1B6 engines, rated at 340 hp each, were equipped with Bendix fuel injection and nitrided cylinders. Supercharged powerplants gave the Model 65 a maximum cruising speed of 214 mph and a range (standard tanks) of 1,070 statute miles. Maximum speed was 239 mph with 1,300 feet per minute rate of climb. Three-blade propellers were standard. The Queen Air boasted a useful load approaching 3,000 pounds and established itself as a fast, comfortable twin that was easy to fly and economical to operate. Although slightly faster than the Model E18S/G18S, still reigning flagships of the Beech corporate fleet, the Queen Air only supplanted the venerable Twin-Beech in the company's marketing strategy. However, the Model 65 represented the future course Beech would take in developing advanced aircraft. Weather radar, remote-

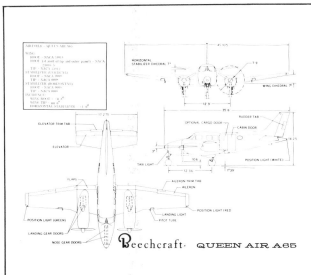

mounted avionics and complete wing/tail surface deice boots, propeller deice and alcohol windshield anti-ice systems were only a few of the many items of optional equipment available for the Queen Air. Wingspan was 45 feet 10 1/2 inches. Jet-assisted takeoff (JATO) units were optional for increased takeoff performance. Deliveries began in late 1959 (1960 model year) and 56 were built the first year. Price: 1960: $126,000 reduced in 1964 to $110,000.

MODEL 65 QUEEN AIR

On February 8, 1960, company test pilot James D. Webber took off from Beech Field in a standard production, fully-equipped Model 65 Queen Air (N110Q) and climbed to an altitude of 34,862 feet, securing a world record for airplanes in the Class C-1.d category. Normal service ceiling of the Queen Air was 27,000 feet, and Webber's demonstration proved that the newest Beechcraft would perform beyond its published figures. Model 65 flown by Webber is illustrated in its record-setting configuration.

Instrument panel of Model 65 Queen Air N110Q used by James D. Webber for altitude record. Typical of the average-equipped Queen Air delivered by Beech, weather radar is installed along with complete avionics equipment for IFR/IMC flight operations.

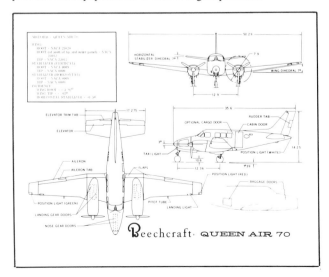

MODEL A65 QUEEN AIR

Basically identical to the earlier Model 65 Queen Air, the Model A65 differed primarily in having a swept tail with dorsal fairing and 214-gallon fuel capacity in rubber bladders. 340 hp Lycoming IGSO-480 engines, useful load of 2,740 pounds and a range of 1,265 statute miles with 45-minute fuel reserves made the A65 the choice of many Queen Air owners. Like the Model 50 Twin Bonanza, Queen Airs used engine exhaust augmenter tubes that automatically controlled engine cooling and eliminated cowl flaps. During climb maximum airflow cooled the engine; during descent, minimum airflow was permitted. Tubes gave the powerful Lycomings a distinctive roar, particularly on takeoff. First produced for the 1967 model year, 29 Model A65 were built followed by four in 1968. In 1968-1969, Beech offered the A65-8200 with a gross weight of 8,200 pounds and 52 were built. A65 was produced from 1967 to 1970. Model A65 illustrated has optional, large fourth cabin window, installed on right side only.

MODEL 70 QUEEN AIR

The Model 70 Queen Air combined 340 hp engines of the Model A65 with Model 80 wings of increased span to create an airplane with high useful load and low operating costs. Introduced in 1969, most Model 70s were built for commuter airline operators under the designation Queen Airliner, seating nine passengers in a high-density configuration. Optional cargo pod installed under the fuselage held 500 pounds of baggage/cargo and a large cargo door could be fitted to make loading/unloading of bulky objects easier. Air conditioning, optional on all Queen Air models, could be added for maximum cabin comfort. Model 70 useful load was a respectable 3,205 pounds and maximum speed 239 mph; cruise speed was 200 mph with a range of 1,265 statute miles (including 45-minute fuel reserve). Rate of climb was 1,375 feet per minute; single-engine rate of climb: 230 feet per minute. Only 35 Model 70 were built before production ended in 1970.

MODEL 73 JET MENTOR

Developed in 1955 to meet a U.S. Air Force and U.S. Navy requirement for a basic jet trainer, Beech designed the Model 73 as a private venture. Using many parts and assemblies already proven on the Beechcraft Model 45 Mentor (T-34A/T34B), the tandem seat, two-place Model 73 was intended to be as economical as possible to buy and operate. First flown on December 18, 1955 by test pilot Tom Gillespie, the Jet Mentor featured complete cockpit air conditioning, dual ejection seats and speed brakes. With a gross weight of approximately 4,500 pounds, the Model 73 had a maximum design speed of 295 mph at 15,000 feet and a stall speed of only 65 mph. Service ceiling was approximately 28,000 feet. Despite good performance and handling qualities, the Jet Mentor lost the lucrative Air Force contract to the Cessna Model 318 that became the T-37 in military service. The Navy evaluated the Jet Mentor and liked it, but ordered the competing Temco jet primarily because of price. Only one Model 73 was built. Note large, clear canopy affording excellent all-round visibility to the pilot and instructor-pilot.

MODEL 76 DUCHESS

In the mid-1970s, general aviation manufacturers produced a group of new, advanced technology light, twin-engine airplanes designed primarily for the multi-engine trainer market. Grumman American designed the Cougar, Piper built the Seminole and Beech Aircraft Corporation flew its PD 289 (Preliminary Design 289) 4-place twin powered by two 180 hp Lycoming O-360 engines. Boasting a large T-tail, PD 289 was redesignated Model 76 and named Duchess in keeping with Beech's family of royal names. Making its initial flight on May 24, 1977 under command of company test pilot Vaughn Gregg, the Duchess featured counter-rotating propellers and a 191 mph maximum speed. Range was 970 statute miles. Bonded, honeycomb structural technology was employed extensively in the Model 76 airframe. Landing gear operation featured an electro-hydraulic powerpack system, with the nose gear retracting forward and the main gear inward. Built at Beech's Liberal, Kansas facility, 72 airplanes were built in 1978 and 213 in 1979. A total of 437 Model 76 Duchess were built before production ended in 1982.

Model 73 Jet Mentor caught in a playful mood above the clouds.

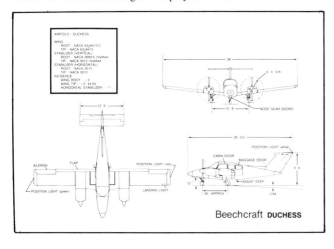

Beechcraft **DUCHESS**

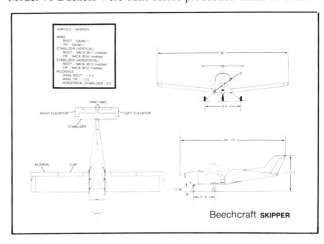

Beechcraft **SKIPPER**

56

MODEL 76 - TURBOCHARGED (EXPERIMENTAL)

In 1979, Beech installed 180 hp TO-360 turbocharged Lycoming engines on a Model 76 Duchess for flight testing. Known unofficially as the Model 76TC, the cowlings were modified to provide extra room for the aft-mounted turbocharger and were larger overall than cowlings of naturally-aspirated, standard production airplanes. First flight was January 31, 1979 with pilot Vaughn Gregg and flight test engineer Bryan Mee on board. A total of 43 flights were made, accumulating 34.4 hours before the 76TC project was cancelled. Last flight was July 10, 1979. Note single, extended exhaust stack of turbocharged Lycoming protruding below cowling.

MODEL 65-80 QUEEN AIR

Introduced in 1962, the Model 65-80 Queen Air featured a swept tail replacing the straight tail of the Model 65, more powerful Lycoming IGSO-540-A1A, fuel-injected, supercharged powerplants rated at 380 hp for takeoff. Gross weight increased to 8,000 pounds and maximum speed was 252 mph with a cruising speed of 230 mph. Model 65-80 had shorter, 45 foot 10 1/2 inch wingspan of Model 65 and was the second version of the Queen Air to be produced. First flight of Model 65-80 was August 25, 1961.

MODEL 65-B80/B80A QUEEN AIR ▶

Beech's continuing refinement of the Queen Air series resulted in the Model 65-B80 of 1966. Equipped with 380 hp Lycoming IGSO-540-A1A engines and three-blade propellers, the B80 cost $182,000 at the factory and gave its owner a lot for the money. Useful load was the highest of any Queen Air produced, at 3,760 pounds. Gross weight was 8,800 pounds. Model 65-B80 featured the longer wingspan of the 80 and A80 series and had a maximum speed of 248 mph, two-engine rate of climb 1,275 feet per minute and single-engine rate of climb was 265 feet per minute. With one engine inoperative the service ceiling was 11,800 feet. In 1968 Beech offered the Model 65-B80A equipped with 360 hp Lycoming IGSO-540-A1D engines. Weights and performance remained basically identical to Model 65-B80 Queen Air. By 1971, only the Model 65-B80 remained in production and continued to be produced until 1977 as an alternative airplane to the turboprop King Air series.

MODEL 77 SKIPPER

Designed primarily as a basic trainer for Beech's Aero Center flying clubs, the Skipper started life as PD 285 in 1974. A new technology GA(W)-1 airfoil was selected for the wing and a T-tail empennage was eventually chosen (flight testing was also done with a conventional tail for comparison) to give good pitch control at low speeds and positive recovery from intentional spins, which the airplane was approved to perform. A Lycoming 0-235-L2C, four-cylinder opposed engine developing 115 hp gave the Skipper a maximum speed of 121 mph and a range of 475 statute miles. Fuel capacity was 29 gallons useable. Maximum takeoff gross weight was 1675 pounds. Model 77 began teaching Aero Center fledglings to fly in 1979, when 47 airplanes were produced. 312 Skippers were built from 1979-1981. Model 77 first flight: September 12, 1978. Pilot: Vaughn Gregg.

MODEL 65-A80 QUEEN AIR

Second version of the 65-80 Queen Air was the Model 65-A80, produced from 1964 to 1966. Primary differences from the Model 65-80 were increased wingspan from 45 feet 10 1/2 inches to 50 feet three inches, stronger airframe structure to accept a higher gross weight of 8,500 pounds and fuel capacity increased by 34 gallons. The 65-80's 380 hp engines were retained and maximum speed was 252 mph with a cruising speed of 212 mph at 65% power setting. Beech also built the Model 65-A80-8800 with 8,800-pound gross weight concurrently with the 8,500-pound A65-A80. Model 65-A80 illustrated is c/n LD-188, built in 1964, one of 45 airplanes produced that year.

MODEL 88 QUEEN AIR

First known as the Model 85 in 1962, then Model 85D in late 1963, the Model 88 drew heavily on the Model 90 King Air's technology for its pressurization system, and actually flew 18 months after the King Air's maiden flight 1-24-64. First flown on July 2, 1965 the Model 88 was basically a piston-powered version of the Model 90, offered to customers as an alternative to the more expensive Pratt & Whitney PT6-20 turboprop-powered A90 King Air. Priced at $259,500, the pressurized Queen Air cruised at 221 mph and had a service ceiling of 27,000 feet and range of 1,200 statute miles. The 88's pressurization system provided a cabin altitude of 8,000 feet at 16,500 feet. Deliveries began in 1965, with four produced. 34 were built in 1966...the largest single quantity. Possessing good performance, luxury equal to that of the Model 90 King Air and a much lower price, the Model 88 fell prey to the increasing demand for turboprop-powered Beechcraft airplanes. Last Model 88 built was c/n LP-47, the only pressurized 88 manufactured in 1969. The final engineering effort for the pressurized Queen Air was the Model A88 with 400 hp Lycoming engines. Model 88 c/n LP-27 served as the testbed for the A88, which made its first flight March 28, 1966 with test pilot Bob Hagan. Although performance increases were promising, Beech elected not to pursue the A88 because of the A90 King Air's superior performance and customer acceptance. No Model A88s were produced and LP-27 was converted to A90 King Air configuration. Model 88 illustrated displays circular cabin windows that identify the pressurized Queen Air. Engines were 380 hp Lycoming ISGO-540-series used on non-pressurized Model 80 Queen Air.

MODEL 65-90 KING AIR (PROTOTYPE)

Originally conceived in 1961 as the Model 120, a 300 mph executive transport, the Model 90 King Air was formally announced on July 14, 1963 and went aloft for the first time on January 24, 1964. Beech engineers grafted Pratt & Whitney PT6A-6 free-turbine, reverse-flow turboprop powerplants onto the basic Queen Air airframe (modified to accept pressurization) and created the King Air. Model 90's engine installation closely resembled that of the first turboprop-powered Beechcraft, the Model 87, c/n LG-1, that had been test flying with PT6A-6 engines on its modified Queen Air airframe since May, 1963. The airplane accumulated almost 10 months of flight testing before delivery to Fort Rucker, Alabama in March, 1964 under the designation NU-8F. The King Air Model 90's wingspan was 45 feet 10 1/2 inches, length 35 feet six inches and stood 14 feet 2 1/2 inches high at the tip of its swept tail. Gross weight was 9,300 pounds with a fuel capacity of 122 gallons in nacelle tanks and 262 gallons in wing tanks. The PT6A-6 engines were rated at 550 shp for takeoff, 500 shp continuous and delivered 1192 pound-feet of torque to the three-blade, constant-speed full-feathering, non-reversible propellers. Cabin pressurization was provided by a single Roots-type supercharger mounted in the left nacelle. Normal pressurization was limited to 3.4 psid with a pressure relief valve adjusted to 4.0 psid to prevent overpressurization. Maximum speed was 280 mph. The first King Air, N5690K, is illustrated.

Since the 1960's, Japan Airlines has used Queen Airs, Model 18s, and C-90A King Airs for advanced multi-engine training.

58

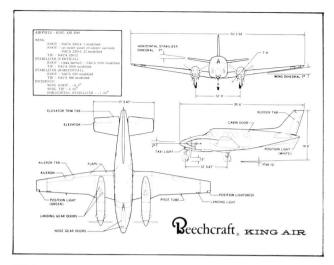

MODEL 90/A90/B90 KING AIR

The Beechcraft Model 90 King Air was enthusiastically received by every corporation and company that took delivery of their new jetprop executive transport. Pilots quickly became accustomed to the simplified operation of the quiet, fuel-efficient PT6A-6 turbine engines and appreciated the airplane's ease of handling, climb and cruise performance. 112 Model 90 King Airs were produced from 1964 to 1966, when production shifted to the Model A90. Equipped with PT6A-20 powerplants rated at 550 shp for takeoff, 538 shp for climb and 495 shp for cruise, the A90 featured an improved pressurization system capable of operating at a maximum differential of 4.6 psid, providing sea level conditions up to more than 10,000 feet and an 8,000-foot cabin altitude above 21,000 feet. A90 first flight was November 5, 1965 and were the first production King Airs to feature reversing propellers. 206 Model A90 were built. The Model B90 flew April 13, 1967 and entered production in 1968 with improved airframe systems and 550 (takeoff) shp PT6A-20 engines. 184 B90 were built before production of the Model C90 began in 1971. Early production Model 90 is illustrated. A90 and B90 were almost identical in appearance to Model 90 King Air.

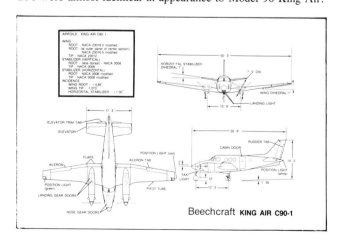

A90-1 - U-21A

The U.S. Army ordered the Model A90 for military duty as the U-21A, Beech designation A90-1. A total of 110 were built from 1966 to 1968. Powered by Pratt & Whitney PT6A-20 engines rated at 550 shp, most of the airplanes eventually served with U.S. forces in Southeast Asia, operated primarily as transports and surveillance aircraft. Non-pressurized, the A90-1 featured square windows and a large cargo door combined with the standard airstair door. In 1968, Beech manufactured the A90-1 for the U.S. Army designated RU-21A (four airplanes) and RU-21D (10 airplanes) for special mission applications. The first production U-21A is illustrated. (Refer to Appendix C, #12)

U.S. Army RU-21E (Beech Model A90-4) in "Guardrail" dress.

A90-1 - U-21G

Designed to accomodate sophisticated equipment for use in electronic countermeasures and communications, 17 of the U-21G version were manufactured by Beech in 1971, with the alternate designation of A90-1. Constructor numbers were c/n LM-125 - LM-141. Note unusual antenna display above and below fuselage. Cylindrical objects on wingtips are not tip tanks for fuel but pods for electronic equipment. Beech also produced the A90-2 (RU-21B, 3 airplanes) and the A90-3 (RU-21C, two airplanes) for special mission applications with the U.S. Army. All five aircraft were built in 1967.

A90-4 - RU-21E/RU-21H ▲

Built in 1971, the A90-4 was designated RU-21E or RU-21H by the U.S. Army and used for electronic surveillance and related missions. Engines were PT6A-28 rated at 620 shp. Gross weight was 10,900 pounds. 16 were built, c/n LU-1 -LU-16.

MODEL C90/C90-1 KING AIR

The next step in King Air progression was the 1971 Model C90, with a wingspan of 50 feet three inches (same as Model 80-series Queen Air) and PT6A-20A turboprop engines developing 550 shp for takeoff. Some early production C90 were equipped with PT6A-6 engines that were modified to PT6A-6/C20 that was equivalent to the -20A powerplant. Empty weight was 5,680 pounds with a gross weight of 9,650 pounds. Seating six comfortably in its pressurized cabin, the C90 cost $399,500 including complete anti-ice/deice equipment and avionics. Maximum cruising speed was 253 mph, initial rate of climb 2,000 feet per minute and the C90 could reach a service ceiling of 25,600 feet. 32 C90 were delivered the first year and a total of 507 were built from 1971 to 1982 when the improved C90-1 entered production. Equipped with PT6A-21 engines rated at 550 shp for takeoff and 538 shp for cruise climb and cruise segments of flight, the C90-1 carried 384 gallons of useable fuel and featured a maximum takeoff weight of 9,650 pounds. Pressurization was increased to 5.0 psid providing a cabin altitude of 6,000 feet at 20,000 feet and 12,000 feet cabin altitude at 30,000 feet. Up to 350 pounds of baggage or remote avionics equipment could be placed in the nose compartment with another 350 pounds of baggage in the aft cabin section, depending on exact arrangement of cabin seats and options installed. Maximum cruising speed: 273 mph with a range of 1,497 statute miles. Model C90 first flight: September 29, 1970.

MODEL C90A KING AIR

The Model C90A incorporated major changes from the earlier Model 90 series, the most salient of these changes being a completely new powerplant package featuring pitot-type cowlings with improved air intake design and the use of tapered exhaust stacks on the two flat-rated, 550 shp UACL PT6A-21 powerplants. Fuel capacity remained at 384 gallons. Maximum takeoff gross weight: 9,650 pounds and maximum operating speed 226 knots IAS (indicated airspeed). C90A deliveries began in 1984 with c/n LJ-1063 and cost $1,347,800 (1986). A higher gross weight C90A was introduced in 1987 beginning with c/n LJ-1138, LJ-1142 and after with 10,160-pound maximum ramp weight, maximum takeoff weight of 10,100 pounds. C90A first flight, c/n LJ-1063: September 1, 1983. Pilot: Jim Dolbee.

Beech introduced the C90B in October, 1991. The newest member of the King Air family featured an upgraded interior with tuned dynamic vibration absorbers strategically located throughout the cabin to reduce airframe vibration. New, dynamically-balanced four-blade propellers and a synchrophasing system further reduced cabin sound levels. The first production C90B illustrated (c/n LJ-1288) was fitted with the 10,000th Pratt & Whitney Canada PT6A turboprop engine delivered to Beech since King Air production began in 1964. PT6A-21 engines rated at 550 shp each powered the C90B. The prototype aircraft's first flight (LJ-1240) was August 28, 1990, flown by Tony Marlow. Beech had converted LJ-1240 from C90A to C90B configuration for certification work. It was reconverted and sold as a C90A.

MODEL E90 KING AIR

Mounting PT6A-28 turboprop engines of 680 shp flat-rated to 550 shp, the 1972 Model E90 King Air was very similar to the Model C90. Pressurization remained the same as C90 at 4.6 psid but performance increased with a cruise speed at 16,000 feet of 285 mph and a service ceiling of 27,620 feet. At maximum range power setting, the E90 could fly 1,870 statute miles. 22 were built in 1972 and a total of 347 E90 were produced from 1972 to 1981 when the last airplane, c/n LW-347 rolled off the assembly line. Model E90 first flight: January 18, 1972.

Early production Model F90 instrument panel is typical of most King Airs, equipped with weather radar, autopilot/flight director, RMI (radio magnetic indicator) and HSI (horizontal situation indicator) and dual nav/com avionics. Warning annunciators are located in padded glareshield, caution and advisory annunciators in lower center-subpanel group to inform crew of system status.

MODEL F90 KING AIR

Conceived as an advanced King Air version using a Model E90 fuselage and wings combined with the Model 200 Super King Air's swept, T-tail empennage, the Model F90 made its first flight on January 16, 1978 with Beech test pilot Marv Pratt at the controls. Intended as a step-up King Air from the E90, the F90 was equipped with two 750 shp Pratt & Whitney PT6A-135 turboprop engines, seated seven to 10 occupants (including crew) and cruised at 307 mph. To reduce noise level, the four-blade, constant-speed, full-feathering, reversible propellers turned at a maximum 1900 rpm or 1500 rpm for cruise operation. Initial rate of climb was 2,380 feet per minute, with a maximum altitude capability of 31,000 feet. Model F90 has the distinction of being the first King Air equipped with Beech's advanced multi-bus electrical system that featured automatic load shedding, five separate buses and solid-state current sensors for ground fault protection and bus isolation. The F90 prototype, c/n LA-1, was converted to experimental Model G90, c/n LE-0. A total of 202 Model F90 were produced from 1979 to 1983 when production transitioned to the Model F90-1.

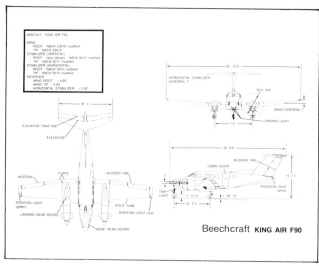

Beechcraft KING AIR F90

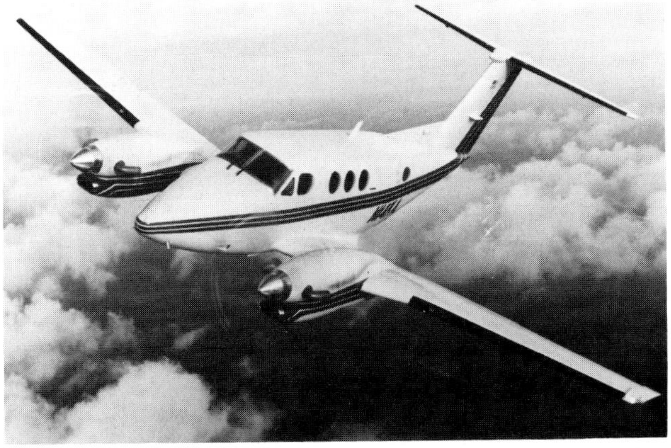

MODEL F90-1 KING AIR

Introduced in the 1983 model year, the Model F90-1 featured pitot-type engine cowl design that improved air intake characteristics, particularly at high altitude. Pratt & Whitney PT6A-135A turboprop powerplants replaced -135 engines of the F90 but were still rated at 750 shp. Wingspan: 45 feet 10 1/2 inches. Main and auxiliary fuel tanks in the wings hold 388 gallons (total) and the auxiliary tanks, located in the wing center section, hold up to 41 gallons of fuel. The first F90-1 was c/n LA-202 in 1983, and a total of 33 airplanes were built from 1983 to 1985. Last F90-1 produced was LA-236. F90-1 first flight (LA-91): January 5, 1981. Pilot: Vaughn Gregg. First production F90-1 test flight (LA-202): December 7, 1982. Pilot: Don Benes, Beech Production Flight Test Department.

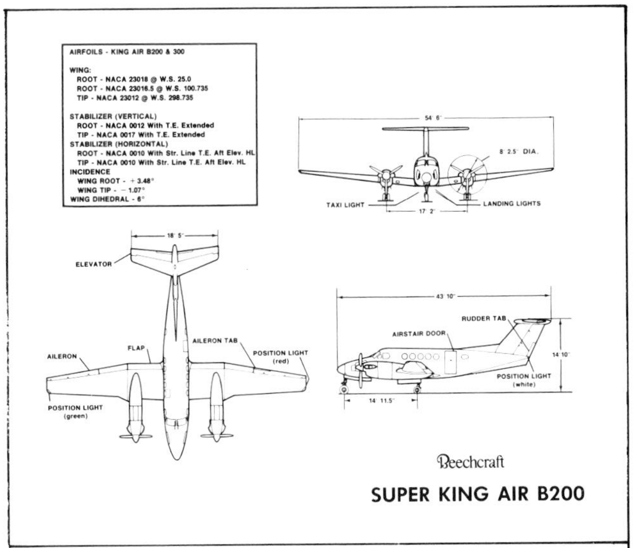

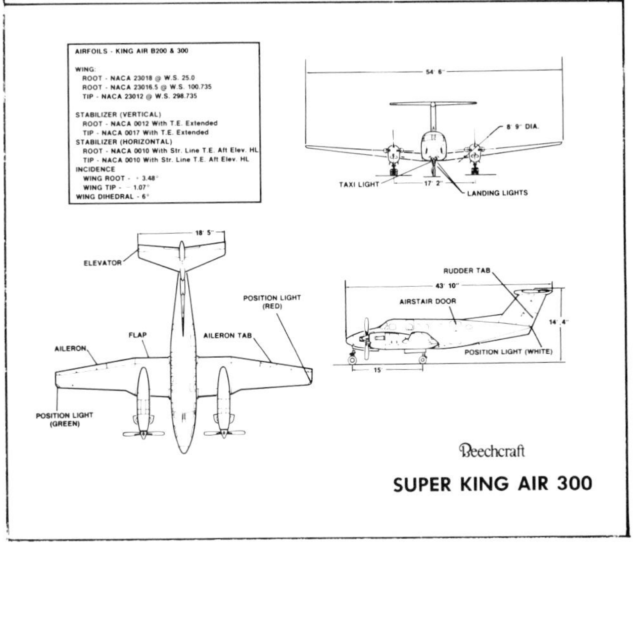

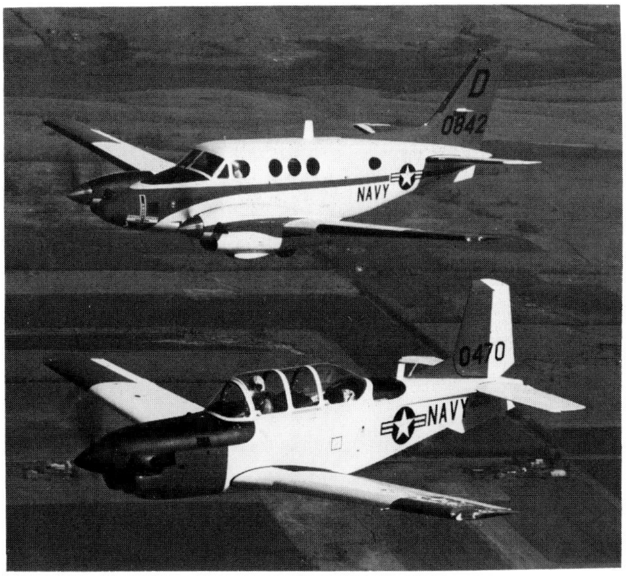

MODEL H90 - T-44A

The U.S. Navy awarded Beech Aircraft Corporation a contract in 1976 that eventually led to 61 Model H90 (not directly equivalent to Model C90 or E90 King Air) advanced, multi-engine pilot trainers designated T-44A. Powered by 550 shp PT6A-34B engines, performance was similar to Model C90 King Air. Maximum ramp weight: 9,710 pounds; maximum takeoff weight: 9,650 pounds. First deliveries occurred in 1977 and the majority of T-44A were assigned to Naval Air Station Corpus Christi, Texas. 13 T-44A were built in 1977: Beech c/n LL-1 - LL-13; Navy serial number s/n 160839 - 160851; 21 were built in 1978: c/n LL-14 - LL-35; Navy s/n 160852 - 160856 and s/n 160967 - 160983; 23 were produced in 1979: c/n LL-36 - LL-58; Navy s/n 160984 - 160986 and s/n 161057 - 161076. The last batch were manufactured in 1980: c/n LL-59 - LL-61; Navy s/n 161077 - 161079. T-44A illustrated flying formation with U.S. Navy T-34C.

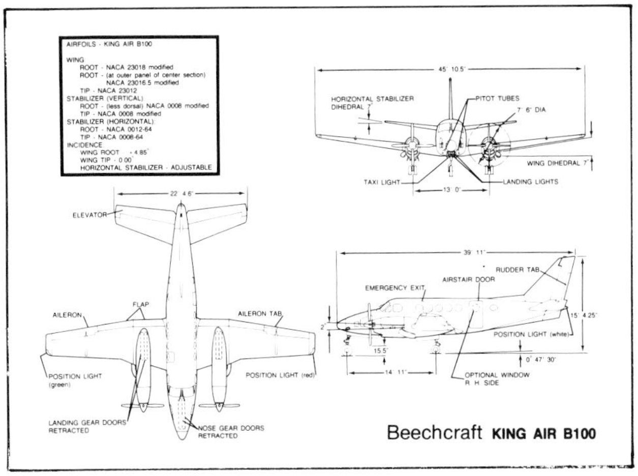

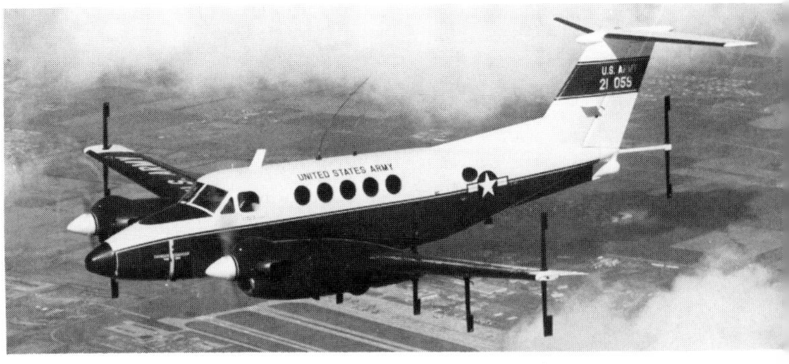

U.S. Army A100-1 (Beech Model 200) equipped for "Guardrail" duty.

MODEL 95 TRAVEL AIR

First flown on August 6, 1956 the Model 95 was designed to fill a gap between the single-engine Model 35 Bonanza and the much larger Model 50 Twin-Bonanza. Seating four in a cabin surrounded by generous window area, the Model 95 was powered by two, four-cylinder Lycoming 0-360-A1A engines developing 180 hp, swinging two-blade, constant-speed, full-feathering propellers. Maximum cruise speed was 200 mph, maximum speed 208 mph and gross weight 4,000 pounds. Service ceiling was 19,300 feet and two-engine rate of climb 1,350 feet per minute. With a fuel capacity of 112 gallons, the Model 95 could fly over 1,400 statute miles and maintained 8,000 feet on one engine at gross weight. Originally dubbed "Badger", the Model 95 had its name changed to "Travel Air" to avoid conflict with the U.S. Air Force, who had already assigned Badger as a code name for the Russian Tupolev TU-16 bomber (Beech was not aware of the military name). Wingspan was 37 feet 10 inches, length 25 feet four inches. 173 Model 95 were built in 1958, the airplane's first production year, followed by 128 in 1959. 1958 Model 95 is illustrated. Note baggage door on right side of fuselage and retracted assist step.

MODEL B95/B95A TRAVEL AIR

By 1960, after only two years of production, the Model 95 had established itself as one of the most popular light twin-engine airplanes available, and Beech introduced the B95 Travel Air to help ensure continued success. The cabin was lengthened 19 inches for more aft cabin room, the horizontal stabilizer and elevators received more area for improved pitch control and the vertical stabilizer incorporated a graceful dorsal fairing that improved overall appearance. Gross weight increased by 100 pounds to 4,100 while useful load went up to 1,465 pounds. Priced at $51,500 each, 150 B95 were built. The Model B95A debuted in 1961, boasting fuel-injected 180 hp Lycoming IO-360-B1A engines, and a higher maximum speed of 210 mph. 81 B95A were produced. Price at the factory was $49,500.

MODEL D95A TRAVEL AIR

The Model D95A Travel Air for 1963 received the same larger, curved third cabin window that was standard on the A55/B55 Baron. Forward baggage space in the redesigned, more tapered nose section was increased to 19 cubic feet, providing more room for the ever-increasing array of modern avionics available from Beech. Aft cabin baggage limit was increased to 400 pounds but price remained at $49,500. Like earlier Travel Airs, a combustion heater provided cabin heat and the tricycle landing gear was electrically operated. A total of 174 D95A were built.

MODEL E95 TRAVEL AIR

Beech produced only 14 Model E95 Travel Airs, all built in 1968. Minor refinement to the interior, a redesigned exterior paint scheme, new one-piece windshield and pointed propeller spinners were the most salient changes incorporated into one of Beech's most successful airplanes. Customer demand for the more powerful, affordable Model B55 Baron eroded Model E95's clientele and production ended in 1968 when the last 95, c/n TD-721, was built.

Model D95A Travel Air instrument panel. Note center-mounted throttles with mixture controls at right and propeller controls at left, throwover-type control wheel.

▼ MODEL 99/B99 AIRLINER

Beech airplanes such as the Model 18 and Model 70 Queen Airliner had long been used for charter and feeder airline service around the world, but in 1967 Beech unveiled the new Model 99 Airliner powered by two Pratt & Whitney PT6A-20 turboprop engines rated at 550 shp. An extended-fuselage Queen Air was used as a testbed to develop the airframe before turboprop powerplants were installed. The Model 99 seated 15 passengers and a crew of two or could be ordered in an executive version that seated six. A large, double cargo door was optional and often selected by airline operators. First flight of the long-fuselage prototype took place in December, 1965 and first flight with turboprop engines occurred in July, 1966. To accomodate the wide CG (center of gravity) range of the Model 99, the entire horizontal stabilizer was electrically trimmed by the pilot, with elevators acting in the conventional manner for pitch control. A standby electric trim system, geared to operate at 1/3 the speed of the main trim system, provided redundancy. Pulsed tones informed the crew anytime trim was occurring. 99 had a wingspan of 45 feet 10 1/2 inches, length of 44 feet 6 3/4 inches and a gross weight of 10,400 pounds. Maximum cruising speed was 284 mph with a range of 1,000 statute miles. Deliveries began in 1968, and most airplanes were delivered with the optional, removeable cargo pod that held an additional 600 pounds. In 1969 Beech delivered nine Model 99A with derated UACL PT6A-27 engines (550 shp) to the Chilean Air Force replacing its fleet of Beech C-45s. In 1972, the improved Model B99 began production, equipped with 680 shp PT6A-28 engines, 10,900-pound maximum takeoff weight and featuring airframe and systems improvements of the corporate Model A100 King Air. 101 Model 99 were built, 43 Model 99A and only one A99A, with special, decreased capacity fuel system. 18 Model B99 were produced but some 99 and 99A were converted to B99 configuration. Model B99 is illustrated.▼

MODEL C99 AIRLINER

The Model C99 first flight occurred on June 20, 1980 with Beech engineering test pilot Jim Dolbee at the helm. The C99 incorporated a redesigned two-bus electrical system featuring solid-state voltage regulation, improved hydraulic landing gear system and a stronger wing spar structure. Powerplants chosen for the C99 were modular-concept UACL PT6A-36, rated at 715 shp for enhanced high altitude, hot-day performance. Water/methanol injection was optional, the enlarged cargo pod held 600 pounds and maximum takeoff weight was 11,300 pounds. Model C99 was produced at Beech's Selma, Alabama Division. A total of 71 Model C99 were built from 1982 to 1986. Model C99 illustrated is U-50, a Model 99 rebuilt by Beech in 1980 as the C99 prototype.

MODEL 100/A100 KING AIR

Unveiled in May, 1969, the Model 100 ascended the throne as Beech Aircraft Corporation's largest King Air. Designed to accomodate executives in luxury or 13 passengers in commuter airline dress, the Model 100 featured wings, tail and powerplants from the Model 99 married to a fuselage of the same cross-section as the Model 90 King Air but longer in length. First flown on March 17, 1969, the Model 100 mounted two PT6A-28 engines rated at 680 shp for takeoff and 620 shp for cruise, giving the flagship a maximum cruise speed of 287 mph. Gross weight was 10,600 pounds...the highest for any corporate King Air at that time. Fuel capacity was 388 gallons with auxiliary tanks holding 82 gallons. The Model 100's pressurization system was limited to a maximum differential of 4.7 psid and the same electrically-operated horizontal stabilizer trim system used in the Model 99 Airliner was installed on the Model 100 series. 89 airplanes were built from 1969 to 1970. In 1971, the Model A100 King Air replaced the Model 100 on the Beechcraft production lines. Basically an advanced version, the A100 featured a 900-pound increase in maximum takeoff gross weight to 11,500 pounds, carried an additional 96 gallons of fuel that stretched range to 1,542 statute miles at an altitude of 21,000 feet. Four-blade propellers with shorter span improved ground clearance during taxi and landing operations. The A100 cruised through the sky at 271 mph at 21,000 feet and could climb to a service ceiling of 24,850 feet. Model A100 first flight: March 20, 1970. A100 production ended in 1979 after 157 were built. Model A100 is illustrated. Note small wing fences installed to control airflow separation over ailerons at high angle of attack/low airspeeds.

◄ U-21F

The U.S. Army purchased five Model A100 King Airs in 1971 to serve as pressurized transports. Designated U-21F, the Beech constructor numbers were c/n B-95 - c/n B-99, Army serial number s/n 70-15908 - 70-15912. All five were produced and delivered in 1971. Engines were PT6A-28, 680 shp. Second production U-21F is illustrated in standard U.S. Army livery.

MODEL B100 KING AIR

Beech Aircraft Corporation engaged a second-source supplier of engines for the very successful Model A100 King Air in 1974 when Garrett AiResearch TPE-331-6-251B/252 fixed shaft turboprop powerplants were certified on the Model A100 creating the B100 King Air. First flight was March 20, 1975. Beech had already flight-tested Garrett's TPE-series on a company-owned King Air in 1972 as a feasability study on a possible new model with Garrett power. Producing 840 shp flat-rated to 715 shp, the TPE-331 gave the B100 a maximum cruising speed of 306 mph, with a cabin altitude of 8,000 feet at 21,200 feet. Range was 1,501 statute miles. The B100 was produced until 1983. 137 were built.

MODEL 200 SUPER KING AIR

After four years of research and development, Beech introduced the Model 200 Super King Air in 1973. Known as the Model 101 in 1969, the designation became Model 200 and wind tunnel testing of the airplane's most salient feature, a large T-tail, consumed 375 hours. The distinctive T-empennage raised the tail up out of the wing's downwash, allowing the stabilizer and elevator to operate in relatively smooth, undisturbed air. Development accelerated in 1970 and two prototypes (BB-1/BB-2) were constructed, the first flying on October 27, 1972 and the second December 15, 1972. Beech test pilot Bud Francis was in command for both inaugural flights. The Super King Air was powered by two Pratt & Whitney UACL PT6A-41 turboprop engines rated at 850 shp each, and could deliver that power up to 106 degrees F. 544 gallons of fuel were carried in wing/nacelle tanks and two auxiliary tanks located in the wing centersection that was two feet wider than the A100's. Wingspan increased to 54 feet six inches, length 43 feet nine inches and T-tail height 14 feet 11 1/2 inches. With extra power and wingspan, the Model 200's maximum takeoff gross weight was 12,500 pounds, useful load 5,275 pounds and maximum speed 333 mph. Maximum pressurization system differential was increased to 6.0 psid, resulting in a cabin altitude of 6,740 feet at 25,000 feet or a sea level cabin at 13,820 feet. Model 200's cabin seated up to eight in typical King Air surroundings, air conditioning was standard along with complete wing/tail/propeller deice and windshield anti-ice equipment. Tricycle landing gear continued to use tried and proven electro-mechanical system. Certified in December, 1973, initial deliveries of the Super King Air began in February, 1974. The Model 200 proved to be Beech Aircraft Corporation's crowning achievement in the decade of the 1970s, establishing itself as one of the most popular turboprop airplanes in the world. Model 200 illustrated is N200KA, a Beech demonstrator named "The Free Enterprise". Over 830 Model 200's were built from 1974 to 1981.

MODEL B200 SUPER KING AIR

In 1981, the Model B200 Super King Air took over as Beech's top-of-the-line turboprop. Equipped with (UACL) PT6A-42 engines that retained a rating of 850 shp but incorporated improved hot section components that enabled better climb and high altitude performance, cruise speed increased to 312 mph, pressurization differential increased to 6.5 psid and zero fuel weight (maximum weight of airplane with no fuel) was 11,000 pounds. A double-wide cockpit pedestal made flight deck entry/egress easier and many minor improvements were made to the interior. Next major changes to the Super King Air occurred in 1984, when a 3,000 psi hydraulic landing gear system replaced the electro-mechanical installation effective c/n BB-1193 and after; McCauley propellers were installed effective c/n BB-1193.

Model 200 instrument panel illustrates a typically-equipped Super King Air, with digital display avionics, color weather radar and complete autopilot/flight director.

PD 290 (EXPERIMENTAL)

In 1975, Beech used the first Model 200 Super King Air, c/n BB-1, as a testbed for aerodynamic/systems investigations using turbofan engines. Two Pratt & Whitney JT-15D-4 powerplants were installed and PD 290 (Preliminary Design 290) flew for the first time on March 12, 1975 with Beech engineering test pilot Bud Francis in the left seat. PD 290 made its last flight on September 30, 1977, after accumulating 93.3 hours during 103 test flights. ▼

MODEL 200T SUPER KING AIR

In 1976, Beech modified Model 200 Super King Air c/n BB-186 into c/n BT-1, a company demonstrator equipped with 50-gallon wing tip tanks for increased endurance and range. Designed for maritime patrol, special large, bulged observation windows were installed in the aft cabin section, surveillance radar was housed under the fuselage and a lower fuselage fairing accomodated various photographic equipment for reconnaissance purposes. Electronic control and monitoring consoles were installed in the cabin. Able to remain on station for more than eight hours (at recommended power settings), Model 200T was another example of the Beechcraft Super King Air's inherent versatility. A 3,000 psi hydraulic landing gear system became standard effective c/n BT-31 and after, replacing electro-mechanical installation of constructor number BT-1 -BT-30. Model 200T, N2067D is illustrated. Note camera fairing, visible under fuselage, bulged observation windows and streamlined tip tanks. 31 200T were built from 1976 to 1987. All were 200T originally assigned Model 200 constructor numbers, then reassigned BT constructor numbers.

◄ MODEL 200 SUPER KING AIR - C-12A

The first Model 200's to enter military service were c/n BB-3, BB-4 and BB-5 that were converted to A100-1 airplanes for the U.S. Army in 1974. That same year, the Army and U.S. Air Force ordered 20 and 14 Super King Airs respectively to be designated C-12A, Beech designation Model A200. Basically off-the-shelf airplanes, 20 were produced in 1975 (10 Army, 10 USAF), followed in 1976 by 32 airplanes (12 Army, 20 USAF) and 18 for the Army in 1977. In 1978, 20 airplanes were accepted by USAF and were the last C-12A produced. U.S. Air Force (foreground) and U.S. Army Model A200/C-12A are illustrated in original livery.

MODEL 200/B200 SUPER KING AIR – UC-12 SERIES

The U.S. Navy purchased nine Model A200C in 1979 designated UC-12B, c/n BJ-1 – BJ-9, for use as personnel and utility transports for both the Navy and the U.S. Marine Corps. Basically off-the-shelf airplanes, all were equipped with the 52-inch by 52-inch, upward-opening cargo door of the commercial Model 200C. 27 additional airplanes were ordered in 1980, c/n BJ-10 – BJ-36 and another 22 in 1981 and 8 in 1982. A total of 66 UC-12B were produced from 1979 to 1982. A C-12F in service with the U.S. Air Force is illustrated. Variations of the C-12 series have served with every branch of the U.S. armed forces.

MODEL 300/300LW SUPER KING AIR

The Model 300 was certified under Special Federal Aviation Regulation 41C that permitted small, propeller-driven airplanes to exceed 12,500 pounds maximum gross weight if additional airworthiness criteria were met. A Model 200 Super King Air (c/n 343) was used to develop the Model 300's systems and made its first flight in that configuration on October 6, 1981, flown by Bud Francis and George Bromley. First flight of the prototype Model 300 (c/n FA-1) was made on September 3, 1983, flown by Vaughn Gregg. Two PT6A-60A turboprop engines rated at 1,050 shp each powered the 300, housed in pitot-type cowlings with four-blade propellers. Beech offered only the 300LW lightweight version (12,500 pounds gross weight limit) intended for sale in Europe. From 1984 to 1991, 218 300 and 300LW were built. Aircraft illustrated is a Model 300LW, which continues to be delivered to international customers under Part 23 certification or foreign equivalents.

MODEL 350 SUPER KING AIR

In 1990, the Model 350 Super King Air replaced the Model 300. Officially designated as the B300, the airplane was identified as the Model 350 for marketing purposes and was certified to Part 23, through Amendment 34 for Commuter Aircraft category, of the Federal Aviation Regulations and received its type certificate in December, 1989. Powered by two Pratt & Whitney Canada PT6A-60A turboprop engines rated at 1,050 shp each, the 350 featured a fuselage 34 inches longer than the Model 200 and 300 King Airs. Winglets and a completely new interior were highlights of the 350's design. Standard seating included two double-club chair arrangements. Maximum speed: 315 kt. Range: 1,900 n.m. First flight: September 13, 1988, piloted by Bud Francis. ▼

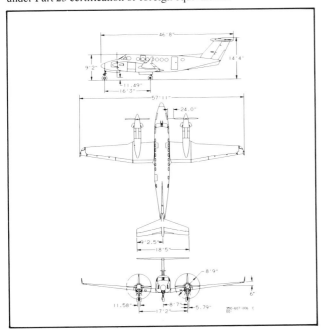

MODEL 38P LIGHTNING - TPE-331-9 (EXPERIMENTAL)
Intended strictly for use as a flying proof-of-concept aircraft to investigate the feasability of a pressurized, turboprop Beechcraft, the Model 38P "Lightning" used a modified Model 58P Baron pressurized fuselage mounted between engine-less wings. The only prototype built, c/n EJ-1, was fitted with a Garrett AiResearch TPE-331-9 rated at 550 shp initially, increased to 630 shp during

MODEL 400 BEECHJET
Mitsubishi's successful Diamond-series executive aircraft product line was purchased by Beech Aircraft Corporation in 1986. Renamed "Beechjet" and assigned the designation Model 400, the seven passenger plus crew of two jet featured a new Beechcraft-designed interior, 732 gallons of fuel carried in two integral (wet cell) wing tanks and two aft fuselage tanks. A pressurization differential of 9.0 psid provided sea level comfort up to 24,000 feet, and a

the flight test program. 38P made its first flight on June 14, 1982 with Beech engineering test pilot Lou Johansen at the controls. A total of 133 flights over a period of 100.7 hours yielded valuable information about the compatability of turboprop engine with the Model 58P airframe. Last flight of the Garrett-powered Lightning was November 14, 1983.

▲MODEL 38P LIGHTNING - PT6A-40 (EXPERIMENTAL)
The PD336 Lightning prototype, c/n EJ-1, was also fitted with a UACL PT6A-40 powerplant flat-rated to 630 shp swinging the same 92-inch diameter, three-blade, reversible propeller used on the earlier Garrett-powered ship. Intended to evaluate performance of the 58P airframe with a Pratt & Whitney powerplant, first flight was March 9, 1984, flown by Lou Johansen. Beech cancelled the Lightning program soon after the March first flight, but engineering flight tests continued in accordance with Federal Aviation Regulations Part 23 to collect as much certification-related information as possible. A total of 68 flights were made over a period of 55.7 hours. Last flight of the 5,800-pound maximum takeoff weight Model 38P was August 8, 1984.

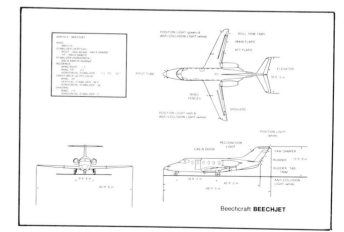

6,400-foot cabin at 41,000 feet. Wingspan: 43.5 feet; length: 48.4 feet; height: 13.8 feet. Range with IFR fuel reserves: 1,530 nautical miles. Powered by two Pratt & Whitney JT-15D-5 engines producing 2,900 pounds thrust, the Beechjet had a maximum speed at 29,000 feet of 530 mph (461 knots) and could be fitted with optional Rohr thrust reversers. Maximum takeoff weight: 15,780 pounds. Beech built more than 60 Model 400 Beechjets.

MODEL 400A/400T

In June, 1990, Beech received FAA certification for the upgraded Beechjet 400A followed by certification of the aircraft's Pro Line 4 Electronic Flight Instrument System, full digital avionic suite developed by Rockwell International's Collins Divisions. With a maximum speed of 468 kt., the 400A featured improvements that included a maximum altitude of 45,000 feet, gross weight increase to 16,100 pounds, increased cabin volume and seating for nine occupants. The lavatory was relocated to the aft cabin. Two Pratt & Whitney JT15D-5 turbofan engines rated at 2,900 pounds static thrust each power the aircraft. Maximum speed: 468 kt. Range: 1,900 n.m. First flight: September 22, 1989, flown by Robert Newsom.

The Model 400T derivative of the Beechjet 400A was selected in 1990 by the U.S. Air Force for its Tanker Transport Training System program. First flight occurred on July 5, 1991 flown by Mike Preston. In January, 1992 Beech delivered the first of 180 Jayhawks (c/n TT-1) scheduled to be built for the service through 1995. A third seat for an instructor or student was added to the cockpit, remote avionics were relocated to the aft cabin, the main landing gear was strengthened and the windscreens were designed for bird strike protection. Two Pratt & Whitney JT15D-5 turbofan engines power the T1-A.

Cockpit of the T1-A Jayhawk shows five-tube EFIS avionic suite including a Multi-Function Display. Other features of the suite include color weather radar, radio tuning units, collision avoidance systems and central diagnostics and maintenance capabilities. ➤

MODEL 1300 AIRLINER

In 1987, Beech Aircraft Corp. modified the Model B200 Super King Air into a 13-seat regional transport designated the Model 1300. Deliveries began in 1988. A total of 14 1300s were built. The first production airplane is illustrated in the livery of Farmington, N.M.-based Mesa Airlines. Note cargo pod beneath fuselage similar to that installed on the C99 airliner.

MODEL 1900/1900C-1

Developed in response to the growing regional airline market, the Model 1900 featured a fuselage much longer than that of the Model B200 Super King Air from which it evolved. The prototype (c/n UA-1) first flew September 3, 1982, piloted by Eric Griffin and Bryan Mee. Powered by two Pratt & Whitney Canada PT6A-65B turboprop engines flat-rated to 1,100 shp, the 1900 had a maximum gross weight of 16,600 pounds, carried 425 gallons of fuel and accommodated 19 passengers. A total of 66 1900s were built before the Model 1900C-1 entered production in 1987. The 1900C-1 featured a wet wing with 670 gallon fuel capacity, increasing range to 1,533 n.m. compared with 794 n.m. for the 1900. Beech delivered 174 1900C-1 airplanes from 1987 to 1991. ▼

MODEL 1900D

First flown on March 1, 1990, by test pilot Lou Johansen, the 19-seat Model 1900D retained the 1900C-1's wet wing, stabilons and tailets but added dual strakes beneath the aft fuselage for increased longitudinal stability. The cabin's 71-inch high center aisle provided stand-up, walk-through space for most passengers, compared with 57 inches for the 1900C-1. In addition, the cabin volume was expanded 28.5 percent, to 640 cubic feet from 498 cubic feet. Powered by Pratt & Whitney Canada PT6A-67 turboprop engines rated at 1,280 shp each, the 1900D has a maximum gross weight 16,950 pounds and a useful load of more than 6,800 pounds. Designed to meet requirements of Part 23 through Amendment 34 of the Federal Aviation Regulations for Commuter aircraft, the 1900D received FAA certification in March, 1991. Maximum speed: 290 kt. Range: 670 n.m. ▼

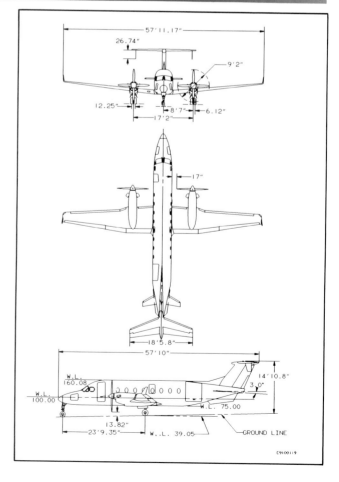

MODEL 1900C-1/C-12J

In 1988, Beech delivered six C-12J versions of the Model 1900C-1 to the Air National Guard for general utility and transport missions.

The supersonic AQM-37C was designed to fly from 1,000 ▲ feet to 80,000 feet and accelerate to Mach 3. Rocket-powered, the Beechcraft target drone could perform realistic combat maneuvering, allowing fighter pilots and ground-based gun crews to experience simulated attack scenarios.

The MQM-107B air defense target system featured turbojet power and could sustain 5g maneuvers during air-to-air combat simulations. The aircraft could tow subtargets on programmable courses for ground gunnery training and was reusable. ▼

MODEL 2000/2000A

Beech Aircraft Corporation's revolutionary Starship 1 business aircraft received FAA certification in June, 1988. The prototype (c/n NC-1) first flew February 15, 1986, piloted by Bud Francis and Thomas Carr. Built primarily of graphite-epoxy and Nomex fibers, the Starship was the most thoroughly tested aircraft in general aviation history. Mounting two Pratt & Whitney Canada PT6A-67 turboprop engines rated at 1,200 shp each in pusher configuration, the airplane achieved a maximum speed of 352 kt. A second prototype (c/n NC-2) flew on June 14, 1986, with Lou Johansen and Thomas Schaffstall on the flight deck. The preproduction Starship (c/n NC-3), made its first flight on January 5, 1987, flown by Thomas Carr and Tony Marlow. In 1991, Beech introduced the 2000A with a six-seat interior, a higher gross weight of 14,900 pounds and increased range of 1,500 n.m. The first production 2000A was c/n NC-21.

Aerial view of the Beechcraft Starship production line shows a fleet of the airplanes under construction. The two aircraft in the foreground have engines installed. ➤

The Starship's flight deck featured a 14-tube EFIS avionic suite for display of navigation, flight and engine systems status. Subpanel and pedestal controls were similar to those installed in the King Air series airplanes.

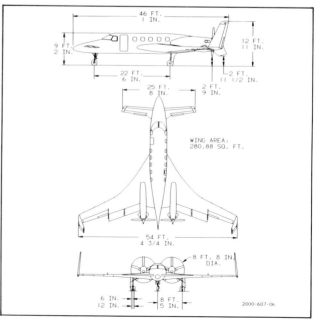

46 FT. 1 IN.

9 FT. 2 IN.

12 FT. 11 IN.

22 FT. 6 IN.

2 FT. 11 1/2 IN.

2 FT. 9 IN.

25 FT. 8 IN.

WING AREA: 280.88 SQ. FT.

54 FT. 4 3/4 IN.

8 FT. 8 IN. DIA.

6 IN. 12 IN.

8 FT. 5 IN.

2000-607-06

APPENDIX A

BEECHCRAFT APPROVED TYPE CERTIFICATES

MODEL	APPROVED TYPE CERTIFICATE	DATE
Model 17 Series		
17R	496	12-20-32
A17F	548	8-08-34
A17FS	577	7-06-35
B17L	560	12-04-34
B17B	560	4-29-36
SB17L	560	11-01-35
B17E	566	5-09-35
B17R	579	7-22-35
C17L	602	4-16-36
C17B	602	4-16-36
SC17L	602	4-16-36
SC17B	602	4-16-36
C17E	615	8-13-36
C17R	604	5-06-36
SC17R	604	11-07-39
D17A	713	5-02-37
D17B	638	9-08-41
D17R	638	5-20-37
D17S	649	7-16-37
SD17S	649	9-08-41
E17L	641	9-01-37
E17B	641	9-08-41
SE17B	641	8-26-38
F17D	689	8-26-38
SF17D	689	6-10-41
G17S	779	10-11-46

NOTE: Military derivatives of Model 17 series:

Model B17R - UC-43H
Model C17B - UC-43G
Model C17L - UC-43J
Model C17R - JB-1, UC-43E
Model D17A - UC-43F
Model D17B - UC-43A
Model D17S - UC-43, UC-43B, GB-1, GB-2
Model D17W - UC-43K
Model E17B - UC-43D
Model F17D - UC-43C

MODEL	APPROVED TYPE CERTIFICATE	DATE
Model 18 Series		
18A	TC 630	3-04-37
S18A	TC 630	10-13-41
18B	TC 656	10-29-37
S18B	TC 656	10-29-37
18D	A 684	6-15-38
S18D	A 684	6-15-38
A18A	A 684	5-07-40
SA18A	A 684	5-07-40
A18D	A 684	5-07-40
SA18D	A 684	5-07-40
18S	A 710	11-2-39
B18S	A 710	4-17-40
C18S	A 757	9-23-44
D18CT	A 770	6-3-47
D18S	A 765	4-26-46
D18C	A 765	7-16-47
E18S	A 765	7-19-54
E18S-9700	A 765	1-19-59
G18S	A 765	10-08-59
H18	A 765	7-11-62

MILITARY DERIVATIVES OF COMMERCIAL MODEL 18 SERIES

C-45G, TC-45G, C-45H, TC-45H, TC-45J, UC-45J,	A 765	3-03-58

MODEL	APPROVED TYPE CERTIFICATE	DATE
SNB-5	A 765	5-10-62
RC-45J, SNB-5P	A 765	1-14-69
JRB-6	A 765	8-30-63
3N, 3NM, 3TM (Canada)	A 765	1-31-68
AT-11, SNB-1	A 2-582	5-02-46

NOTE: Army Air Force AT-11 and Navy SNB-1 were granted Group Two approval #2-582 by Civil Aeronautics Authority on 5-2-46 for licensing as 4PCLM (4 Place Cabin Land Monoplane) with two Pratt & Whitney R-985-SB engines of 450 hp each. All AT-11 and SNB-1 c/n were eligible at 7,835 pound gross weight.

NOTE: The following aircraft were military derivatives of the commercial Model C18S:

C-45, C-45A UC-45B, UC-45F, AT-7, AT-7A, AT-7B, AT-7C, JRB-1, JRB-2, JRB-3, JRB-4, SNB-2, SNB-2C, AT-11	A 757	9-23-44
AT-10	L-12-2	5-14-47

MODEL	APPROVED TYPE CERTIFICATE	DATE
Model 19 - Model 23 - Model 24 Series		
23	A1CE	3-15-60
A23	A1CE	6-07-63
A23A	A1CE	11-05-65
A23-19	A1CE	12-09-65
A23-24	A1CE	3-07-66
A24	A1CE	2-05-70
19A	A1CE	8-31-67
M19A	A1CE	12-09-69
B19	A1CE	2-13-70
B23 (Normal category)	A1CE	12-13-67
B23 (Aerobatic)	A1CE	11-22-68
C23	A1CE	2-13-70
A24R	A1CE	12-23-69
B24R	A1CE	6-18-73
C24R	A1CE	10-01-76

MODEL	APPROVED TYPE CERTIFICATE	DATE
Model 33 - Model 35 Series		
35	A777	3-25-47
A35	A777	7-15-48
B35	A777	12-28-49
C35	A777	1-16-51
35R	A777	6-06-51
D35	A777	1-05-53
E35	A777	1-15-54
F35	A777	1-05-55
G35	A777	12-06-55
H35	3A15	12-01-56
J35	3A15	11-13-57
K35	3A15	10-29-58
M35	3A15	10-02-59
N35	3A15	10-20-61
P35	3A15	10-20-61
S35	3A15	1-03-64
V35	3A15	10-22-65
V35TC	3A15	10-22-65
V35A	3A15	10-22-65
V35A-TC	3A15	10-22-65
V35B	3A15	10-06-69
V35B-TC	3A15	10-06-69
35-33	3A15	11-13-59
35-A33	3A15	11-03-60
35-B33	3A15	10-03-61
35-C33	3A15	12-02-64
35-C33A	3A15	1-20-66

MODEL	APPROVED TYPE CERTIFICATE	DATE
C33A	3A15	1-20-66
D33	A-CE	8-04-66

NOTE: Model D33 was experimental ground attack aircraft issued a Provisonal Type Certificate only. No commercial D33 were built.

MODEL	APPROVED TYPE CERTIFICATE	DATE
E33	3A15	10-10-67
E33A	3A15	10-10-67
E33C	3A15	9-09-68
F33	3A15	10-24-69
F33A	3A15	10-24-69
F33C	3A15	10-24-69
G33	3A15	3-17-71

Model 45 and T-34C Series

MODEL	APPROVED TYPE CERTIFICATE	DATE
A5 (YT-34 prototype)	5A3	7-17-50
A45 (T-34A)	5A3	9-21-53
B45 (T-34 export version)	5A3	9-21-53
D45 (T-34B)	5A3	3-09-60
T-34C	A26CE	8-25-78
T-34C-1	A26CE	12-17-76

Model 36 Series

MODEL	APPROVED TYPE CERTIFICATE	DATE
36	3A15	5-01-68
A36	3A15	10-24-69
A36TC	3A15	12-07-78
B36TC	3A15	1-15-82

Model 50 Series

MODEL	APPROVED TYPE CERTIFICATE	DATE
50	5A4	5-25-51
B50	5A4	7-31-53
C50	5A4	10-13-54
D50	5A4	12-06-55
E50	5A4	12-01-56
D50A	5A4	10-29-57
D50C	5A4	11-13-59
D50E	5A4	11-10-60
D50E (5990 pound MTOW)	5A4	3-21-74
F50	5A4	10-29-57
D50B	5A4	11-10-58
G50	5A4	11-10-58
H50	5A4	11-13-59
N50	5A4	11-13-59
J50	5A4	11-16-60

Model 95-55 And Model 55 Series

MODEL	APPROVED TYPE CERTIFICATE	DATE
95-B55	3A16	9-09-63
95-B55A	3A16	10-31-68
95-B55B	3A16	8-26-64
95-C55	3A16	8-18-65
95-C55A	3A16	10-31-68
D55	3A16	10-17-67
E55	3A16	11-12-69
E55A	3A16	6-16-70

Model 56 Series

MODEL	APPROVED TYPE CERTIFICATE	DATE
56TC	3A16	5-19-67
A56TC	3A16	11-12-69

Model 58 Series

MODEL	APPROVED TYPE CERTIFICATE	DATE
58	3A16	11-19-69
58A	3A16	11-10-70
58P	A23CE	5-21-74
58PA	A23CE	5-12-76
58TC	A23CE	1-23-76
58TCA	A23CE	5-12-76

Model 60 Series

MODEL	APPROVED TYPE CERTIFICATE	DATE
60	A12CE	2-01-68
A60	A12CE	1-30-70
B60	A12CE	10-05-73

Model 65 Series

MODEL	APPROVED TYPE CERTIFICATE	DATE
65	3A20	2-04-59
65-80	3A20	2-20-62
65-A80	3A20	3-26-64
65-A80 (8800 pound MTOW)	3A20	10-22-65
65-B80	3A20	10-22-65
65-88	3A20	9-21-65
65-90	3A20	5-19-64
65-A90	3A20	3-07-66
A65	3A20	11-03-66
A65 (8200 pound MTOW)	3A20	10-09-67
65-A90-1	3A20	4-27-66
65-A90-2	3A20	3-20-69
65-A90-3	3A20	3-20-69
65-A90-4	3A20	12-10-71
70	3A20	11-27-68
B90	3A20	11-14-67
C90	3A20	10-23-70
C90-1	3A20	10-23-70
C90A	3A20	12-1-83
C90B	3A20	10-17-91
E90	3A20	4-13-72
F90	A31CE	5-18-79
F90-1	A31CE	5-18-79
H90	3A20	3-23-77

Model 76

MODEL	APPROVED TYPE CERTIFICATE	DATE
76	A29CE	1-24-78

Model 77

MODEL	APPROVED TYPE CERTIFICATE	DATE
77	A30CE	4-15-80

Model 95 Series

MODEL	APPROVED TYPE CERTIFICATE	DATE
95	3A16	6-18-57
B95	3A16	11-13-59
B95A	3A16	3-09-61
D95A	3A16	5-17-63
D95A	3A16	10-31-68
E95	3A16	10-17-67

Model 99 Series

MODEL	APPROVED TYPE CERTIFICATE	DATE
99	A14CE	5-02-68
99A	A14CE	2-10-69
99A	A14CE	6-10-70
A99	A14CE	2-19-71
A99A	A14CE	2-19-71
B99	A14CE	3-27-72
C99	A14CE	7-27-81

Model 100 Series

MODEL	APPROVED TYPE CERTIFICATE	DATE
100	A14CE	7-24-69
A100	A14CE	5-07-71
A100A	A14CE	11-01-72
A100C	A14CE	12-14-73
B100	A14CE	12-01-75

Model 200 Series

MODEL	APPROVED TYPE CERTIFICATE	DATE
200	A24CE	12-14-73
200C	A24CE	2-21-79
200T	A24CE	12-15-76
200CT	A24CE	2-21-79

MODEL	APPROVED TYPE CERTIFICATE	DATE
A200	A24CE	6-20-75
A200C	A24CE	2-21-79
A200CT	A24CE	4-17-80
B200	A24CE	2-13-81
B200C	A24CE	2-13-81
B200T	A24CE	2-13-81
B200CT	A24CE	2-13-81
Model 300		
300	A24CE	1-24-84
350 (B300)	A24CE	12-12-89
Model 400		
400	A16SW	5-1-86
400A	A16SW	6-20-90
400T	A16SW	11-27-91

NOTE: Mitsubishi Model MU-300-10 was originally certified under ATC A14SW. When Beech Aircraft Corporation obtained the MU-300-10 it received ATC A16SW that incorporates certification for the MU-300-10 and the Model 400 Beechjet. Beechcraft Service Bulletin 2140 permits owners of Mitsubishi airplanes to retrofit their jets to Model 400 configuration.

MODEL	APPROVED TYPE CERTIFICATE	DATE
Model 1900		
1900	A24CE	11-22-83
1900D	A24CE	3-19-91
Model 2000		
2000	A38CE	6-14-88

APPENDIX B

The following compilation details commercial Beechcraft production from 1932 through 1987. Four major segments are presented: model, year produced, constructor number (serial number) and total airplanes built during each model year. Information is presented in numerical order by model.

Additional information regarding military production of certain Beechcraft models is included with the commercial production list. Beech constructor numbers were issued consecutively (regardless of model or type) from 1932 until 1945, when each model was given a discrete identity code.

The Model 17 series listing presents total airplanes produced per calendar year and constructor numbers only where information is known to be accurate and verifiable. Model 18 listing indicates total aircraft delivered per year, not total produced. Information for this listing was procured from official Beech Aircraft Corporation files.

COMMERCIAL PRODUCTION/DELIVERIES - 1932-1942

MODEL	YEAR	CONSTRUCTOR NUMBER	TOTAL DELIVERED
17R	1932	1	0
17R	1933	1	1
17R	1934	2	1
A17F	1934	5	1
A17FS	1934	11	1
B17B	1934	20	1
B17E	1935	22, 49, 51	3
B17L	1934	3, 4, 6-10, 12-21	16
B17L	1935	23-49	26
B17L	1936	58-61	4
B17R	1935	38, 50, 52-56	7
B17R	1936	63-66, 68-72	9
C17L	1936	83, 84, 100, 105, 107, 109	6

MODEL	YEAR	CONSTRUCTOR NUMBER	TOTAL DELIVERED
C17L	1937	124	1
C17R	1936	73-77, 79-82, 113, 114	11
C17R	1937	115, 116, 118-120, 122	6
SC17R	1936	113	1
C17B	1936	67, 84-99, 101-104, 106, 108, 110-112	25
C17B	1937	121, 123, 125-135	13
SC17B	1936	99	1
C17E	1936	78	1
C17E	1937	117	1

NOTE: C17E c/n 78/117 sold to Tokyo Hikoki Seisaku-Jo in Japan and assembled there under supervision of Beechcrafter Virgil H. Adamson in 1937. Aviation historian Richard M. Bueschel states that 20 C17E were built by the Japanese firm under license from Beech Aircraft Company between 1937-1940.

MODEL	YEAR	CONSTRUCTOR NUMBER	TOTAL DELIVERED
E17B	1937	138-145, 149-160, 162, 163, 189-196	30
E17B	1938	197, 198, 204-210, 212, 213, 219, 227, 228, 231-234, 251	19
E17B	1939	274, 280, 336	3
E17B	1940	388	1
SE17B	1937	160	1
SE17B	1938	210, 227	2
SE17B	1939	280	1
E17L	1937	161	1
F17D	1938	211, 225, 226, 229, 240-250, 252, 255	18
F17D	1939	256-262, 270-273, 275-277, 281-283, 307-312, 330-335, 337-339	32
F17D	1940	389-394, 410	7
F17D	1941	412	1
SF17D	1941	414	1
F17D	1942	413	1
D17A	1939	305, 356-361, 363	8
D17A	1940	Not Produced	0
D17R	1937	137, 148, 166, 167, 180-182, 184, 188	9
D17R	1938	214, 215, 217, 218, 235-237, 253	8
D17R	1939	278, 289, 313, 325, 326, 328, 329	7
D17R	1940	397, 405	2
D17S	1937	147, 165, 168, 179, 183, 185-187	8
D17S	1938	199-203, 216, 217, 238, 239, 254	10
D17S	1939	263, 264, 279, 284-288, 295-304, 306, 314, 327, 354, 355, 362	24
SD17S	1939	279	1
D17S	1940	385-387, 395, 396, 398-404, 406-408	16
D17S	1941	415-424	10
D17S	1942	Not Produced	0
D17W	1937	164	1

NOTE: Two D17W were built, but only c/n 164 was delivered as a D17W. The first D17W was c/n 136, built in February, 1937. Reengined before delivery with Wright R-975 of 420 hp as D17R.

MODEL	YEAR	CONSTRUCTOR NUMBER	TOTAL DELIVERED
18A	1937	62	1
18A	1940	291	1
S18A	1937	172	1
18B	1937	170, 171	2
18B	1938	174	1
S18B	1937	173	1
18D	1938	175, 176, 169, 220	4
18D	1939	221, 223, 224, 265, 267, 268	6
S18D	1938	177, 178	2
18S	1939	266, 269, 294	3
18S	1940	292, 316, 430, 431, 433, 434	6
18R	1940	321, 376-380	6
C18S	1940	432	1
C18S	1941	445	1
A18A	1940	290	1

NOTE: By late 1941 when commercial production ceased because of the war effort, Beech had produced approximately 383 airplanes, comprised of 270 Model 17 series and 113 Model 18 series. Of the Model 17 series, 61 F17D were built, followed by 69 D17S, 57 E17B, 44 B17L and 39 C17B. The majority of military Model 18 produced were C-45 and F-2 versions of the Model C18S and B18S respectively.

MODEL	YEAR	CONSTRUCTOR NUMBER	TOTAL DELIVERED

BEECHCRAFT COMMERCIAL PRODUCTION - 1945 - 1987

Model 18 Series

MODEL	YEAR	CONSTRUCTOR NUMBER	TOTAL DELIVERED
D18S	1945	A-1 - A-37	37
D18S	1946	A-38 - A-333	296
D18S	1947	A-334 - A-408	75
D18S	1948	A-409 - A-476	68
D18S	1949	A-477 - A-519	43
D18S	1950	A-520 - A-551	32
D18S	1951	A-552 - A-673	122
D18S	1952	A-674 - A-864	191
D18S	1953	A-865 - A-995	131
D18S	1954	A-996 - A-1019	24
D18S	1956	A-1020 - A-1028	9
D18S	1957	A-1029 - A-1035	7

Model Super E18S Series

MODEL	YEAR	CONSTRUCTOR NUMBER	TOTAL DELIVERED
E18S	1955	BA-1 - BA-112	112
E18S	1956	BA-113 - BA-226	114
E18S	1957	BA-227 - BA-327	101
E18S	1958	BA-328 - BA-402	75
E18S*	1959	BA-403 - BA-433, BA-435 - BA-460	57

*NOTE: 1959 E18S c/n with 9,700-pound gross weight.

MODEL	YEAR	CONSTRUCTOR NUMBER	TOTAL DELIVERED
E18S	1960	BA-497	1

Model Super G18S Series

MODEL	YEAR	CONSTRUCTOR NUMBER	TOTAL DELIVERED
G18S	1960	BA-434, BA-461 - BA-496, BA-498 - BA-551	91
G18S	1961	BA-552 - BA-562, BA-564 - BA-579, BA-581 - BA-597	44
G18S*	1961	BA-563	1

*NOTE: BA-563 had 9,150-pound gross weight.

MODEL	YEAR	CONSTRUCTOR NUMBER	TOTAL DELIVERED
G18S	1962	BA-598 - BA-617	20

Model Super H18 Series

MODEL	YEAR	CONSTRUCTOR NUMBER	TOTAL DELIVERED
H18	1963	BA-580, BA-618 - BA-650	34
H18	1964	BA-651 - BA-711	61
H18	1965	BA-712 - BA-734	23
H18	1966	BA-735 - BA-742	8
H18	1967	BA-743 - BA-752	10
H18	1968	BA-753 - BA-755	3
H18	1969	BA-756 - BA-762	7
H18	1970	BA-763 - BA-765	3

Model 19 - Model 23 - Model 24 Series

MODEL	YEAR	CONSTRUCTOR NUMBER	TOTAL DELIVERED
23	1963	M-1, M-2, M-4 - M-554	553

NOTE: These aircraft designated "Musketeer".

MODEL	YEAR	CONSTRUCTOR NUMBER	TOTAL DELIVERED
A23	1965	M-3, M-555 - M-900	346

NOTE: These aircraft designated "Musketeer II".

MODEL	YEAR	CONSTRUCTOR NUMBER	TOTAL DELIVERED
A23A	1966	M-901 - M-994	94
A23A	1967	M-995 - M-1068	74
A23A	1968	M-1069 - M-1094	26
B23	1968	M-1095 - M-1162	68
B23	1969	M-1163 - M-1284	122
C23	1970	M-1285 - M-1290, M-1292 - M-1297, M-1292 - M-1297, M-1299, M-1300, M-1303	15
C23	1971	M-1291, M-1298, M-1301, M-1302, M-1304 - M-1361	62

NOTE: A23A/B23/C23 series designated "Musketeer Custom III".

MODEL	YEAR	CONSTRUCTOR NUMBER	TOTAL DELIVERED
C23	1972	M-1362 - M-1412, M-1415, M-1419 - M-1423, M-1439, M-1447	56

MODEL	YEAR	CONSTRUCTOR NUMBER	TOTAL DELIVERED
C23	1973	M-1413, M-1414, M-1416- M-1418, M-1420 - M-1422, M-1424 - M-1438, M-1440 - M-1446, M-1448 - M-1490	73
C23	1974	M-1491 - M-1585, M-1587 - M-1599	108
C23	1975	M-1586, M-1600 - M-1726, M-1728 - M-1747	148
C23	1976	M-1727, M-1748 - M-1874, M-1876 - M-1879	132
C23	1977	M-1875, M-1880 - M-1970, M-1972 - M-1979	100
C23	1978	M-1971, M-1980 - M-2085, M-2087 - M-2092	113
C23	1979	M-2086, M-2093 - M-2223, M-2225 - M-2233	141
C23	1980	M-2224, M-2234 - M-2292	60
C23	1981	M-2293 - M-2341	49
C23	1982	M-2342 - M-2368	26
C23	1983	M-2369 - M-2392	24

NOTE: Model C23 from 1972 - 1983 designated "Sundowner 180".

MODEL	YEAR	CONSTRUCTOR NUMBER	TOTAL DELIVERED
A23-19	1966	MB-1 - MB-166	166
A23-19	1967	MB-167 - MB-288	122
19A	1968	MB-289 - MB-392	104
19A	1969	MB-393 - MB-460	68
M19A	1969	MB-461 - MB-480	20
B19	1970	MB-481 - MB-493	13
B19	1971	MB-494 - MB-520	27
B19	1972	MB-521 - MB-557	37
B19	1973	MB-558 - MB-621	64
B19	1974	MB-622 - MB-715, MB-717 - MB-730 *	107

*NOTE: c/n MB-723 not built; replaced by c/n MB-623.

MODEL	YEAR	CONSTRUCTOR NUMBER	TOTAL DELIVERED
B19	1975	MB-716, MB-731 - MB-778	49
B19	1976	MB-779 - MB-813, MB-815, MB-816	37
B19	1977	MB-814, MB-817 - MB-865	50
B19	1978	MB-866 - MB-905	40

NOTE: Model B19 from 1972 - 1978 designated "Sport 150".

MODEL	YEAR	CONSTRUCTOR NUMBER	TOTAL DELIVERED
A23-24	1966	MA-1 - MA-122	122
A23-24	1967	MA-123 - MA-272	150
A23-24	1968	MA-273 - MA-335	63
A23-24	1969	MA-336 - MA-363	28
A24	1970	MA-364 - MA-368	5

NOTE: 1966-1967 A23-24 designated "Musketeer Super".
1968-1969 A23-24 designated "Musketeer Super III".
1970 A24 designated "Musketeer Super". The following list contains c/n for fixed-gear Model A23-24 and A24 that were equipped at the factory with 200 hp Lycoming engines and two-blade, constant-speed propellers. Only 86 airplanes were produced in this configuration:
Model A23-24 - MA-1, MA-85, MA-188, MA-189, MA-190 - MA-192, MA-195 - MA-199, MA-201, MA-210, MA-212, MA-214 - MA-216, MA-219, MA-222, MA-227 - MA-230, MA-236, MA-240, MA-243, MA-246 - MA-248, MA-254, MA-259, MA-260, MA-263, MA-266 - MA-268, MA-280, MA-283, MA-287 - MA-295, MA-297, MA-298, MA-301 - MA-304, MA-306, MA-310 - MA-312, MA-314 - MA-316, MA-318, MA-326, MA-329 - MA-331, MA-334, MA-337, MA-339 - MA-342, MA-344 - MA-346, MA-349, MA-352 - MA-355, MA-357, MA-358, MA-360, MA-362, MA-363.
Model A24: MA-366.

MODEL	YEAR	CONSTRUCTOR NUMBER	TOTAL DELIVERED
A24R	1970	MC-2 - MC-21, MC-24 - MC-38, MC-40, MC-41, MC-44 - MC-47, MC-49 - MC-62, MC-66, MC-67, MC-69, MC-70	59
A24R	1971	MC-22, MC-23, MC-39, MC-42, MC-43, MC-48, MC-63 - MC-65, MC-68, MC-71 - MC-95	35
A24R	1972	MC-96 - MC-150	55
B24R	1973	MC-152 - MC-190	39
B24R	1974	MC-191 - MC-292, MC-294 - MC-304	113
B24R	1975	MC-293, MC-305 - MC-381, MC-383 - MC-385	81
B24R	1976	MC-382, MC-386 - MC-448, MC-450, MC-451	66
C24R	1977	MC-449, MC-452 - MC-532, MC-534 - MC-536	85
C24R	1978	MC-533, MC-537 - MC-619	84
C24R	1979	MC-620 - MC-688, MC-690 - MC-701	81
C24R	1980	MC-689, MC-702 - MC-740	40

MODEL	YEAR	CONSTRUCTOR NUMBER	TOTAL DELIVERED
C24R	1981	MC-741 - MC-764	24
C24R	1982	MC-765 - MC-782	18
C24R	1983	MC-783 - MC-795	13

NOTE: 1972 - 1983 A24R/B24R/C24R designated "Sierra 200".

Model 25	1940	U.S. Army Air Force	1

Original prototype Model 25 destroyed on May 5, 1941. Not rebuilt.

Model 26	1941	U.S. Army Air Force	1,771

Followup design of Model 25. Designated AT-10. Military production only.

Model 28	1945	U.S. Army Air Force	2

NOTE: Model 28 became military XA-38 "Grizzly" ground attack aircraft. Only two were built, both experimental prototypes.

Model 33 Series

MODEL	YEAR	CONSTRUCTOR NUMBER	TOTAL DELIVERED
35-33	1960	CD-1 - CD-224, CD-233, CD-234, CD-236, CD-241, CD-246 - CD-250	233
35-A33	1961	CD-225 - CD-232, CD-235, CD-237 - CD-240, CD-242, CD-245, CD-251 - CD-387	154
35-B33	1962	CD-388 - CD-587	200
35-B33	1963	CD-588 - CD-724	137
35-B33	1964	CD-725 - CD-811	87
35-B33	1965	CD-812, CD-813	2
35-C33	1965	CD-814 - CD-970	157
35-C33	1966	CD-971 - CD-981, CD-983 - CD-1056	85
35-C33	1967	CD-1057 - CD-1118	62
35-C33A	1966	CE-1 - CE-102	102
35-C33A	1967	CE-103 - CE-179	77
E33	1968	CD-1119 - CD-1199	81
E33	1969	CD-1200 - CD-1234	35
F33	1970	CD-1235 - CD-1254	20
G33	1972	CD-1255 - CD-1299	45
G33	1973	CD-1300 - CD-1304	5

NOTE: CD-1305 - CD-1325 changed to F33C at factory.

E33A	1968	CE-180 - CE-235	56

NOTE: CE-236 - CE-248 changed to E33C at factory.

E33A	1969	CE-249, CE-250, CE-260, CE-264 - CE-268, CE-270 - CE-289	29

NOTE: CE-251 - CE-255, CE-257 - CE-259, CE-261 - CE-263, CE-269 changed to E33C at factory. The following G33 and E33A c/n were changed to E33C and F33C at the factory. Old c/n shown in parentheses. From c/n CJ-52 and after no E33A or G33 were converted to F33C configuration.

1968 - E33A to E33C conversion - 13 airplanes:

CJ-1 (CE-236), CJ-2 (CE-237), CJ-3 (CE-238), CJ-4 (CE-239), CJ-5 (CE-240), CJ-6 (CE-241), CJ-7 (CE-242), CJ-8, (CE-243), CJ-9 (CE-244), CJ-10 (CE-245), CJ-11 (CE-246), CJ-12 (CE-247), CJ-13 (CE-248)

1969 - E33A to E33C conversion - 12 airplanes:

CJ-14 (CE-251), CJ-15 (CE-252), CJ-16 (CE-253), CJ-17 (CE-254), CJ-18 (CE-255), CJ-19 (CE-257), CJ-20 (CE-258), CJ-21 (CE-259), CJ-22 (CE-261), CJ-23 (CE-262), CJ-24 (CE-263), CJ-25 (CE-269)

F33A	1970	CE-290 - CE-315	26
F33A	1971	CE-316 - CE-349	34
F33A	1972	CE-350 - CE-401	52
F33A	1973	CE-402 - CE-464	63
F33A	1974	CE-465 - CE-535	71
F33A	1975	CE-536 - CE-611	76
F33A	1976	CE-612 - CE-673	62
F33A	1977	CE-674 - CE-743	70
F33A	1978	CE-744 - CE-815	72

MODEL	YEAR	CONSTRUCTOR NUMBER	TOTAL DELIVERED
F33A	1979	CE-816 - CE-883	68
F33A	1980	CE-884 - CE-928	45
F33A	1981	CE-929 - CE-977	49
F33A	1982	CE-978 - CE-1011	36
F33A	1983	CE-1014 - CE-1023	10
F33A	1984	CE-1024, CE-1025, CE-1027 - CE-1032	8
F33A	1985	CE-1026, CE-1033 - CE-1071,	40
F33A	1986	CE-1072 - CE-1101	29
F33A	1987	CE-1102 - CE-1206	104
F33A	1988	CE-1207 - CE-1306	100
F33A	1989	CE-1307 - CE-1425	119
F33A	1990	CE-1426 - CE-1549	124
F33A	1991	CE-1550 - CE-1639	90
F33A	1992	CE-1640	
F33C	1970	CJ-26 - CJ-30	5
F33C	1988-1991		Not built

NOTE: CJ-26 - CJ-30 standard production F33C.

1973 - G33 to F33C conversion - 9 airplanes:
CJ-31 (CD-1305), CJ-32 (CD-1306), CJ-33 (CD-1307), CJ-34 (CD-1308), CJ-35 (CD-1309), CJ-36 (CD-1310), CJ-37 (CD-1311), CJ-38 (CD-1312), CJ-39 (CD-1313)

1974 - G33 to F33C conversion - 12 airplanes:
CJ-40 (CD-1314), CJ-41 (CD-1315), CJ-42 (CD-1316), CJ-43 (CD-1317), CJ-44 (CD-1318), CJ-45 (CD-1319), CJ-46 (CD-1320), CJ-47 (CD-1321), CJ-48 (CD-1322), CJ-49 (CD-1323), CJ-50 (CD-1324), CJ-51 (CD-1325)

NOTE: CJ-31 - CJ-51 sold to Iran.

F33C	1974	CJ-52 - CJ-63	11

NOTE: CJ-52 - CJ-63 standard production F33C.

F33C	1975	CJ-64 - CJ-102	39
F33C	1976	CJ-103 - CJ-128	26
F33C	1977	CJ-129	1
F33C	1978	CJ-130 - CJ-148	19
F33C	1979	CJ-149 - CJ-155	7
F33C	1986	CJ-156 - CJ-178*	22

*NOTE: CJ-156 - CJ-176 delivered to Mexican Air Force. CJ-177 and CJ-178 were commercial deliveries.

F33C	1987	CJ-179 and after	

Model 35 Series

35	1947	D-1 - D-1209	1196*

*NOTE: The following c/n were reworked by Beech in 1951 as a service to owners of Model 35 Bonanzas who desired to update their airplanes. Modifications included structural changes to empennage, wings and fuselage; gross weight increased to 2,650 pounds; remanufactured Continental E-185-11 engine (takeoff power limited to 196 hp). These airplanes received additional improvements found on the Model B35 and C35 Bonanza but retained the Model 35's tubular steel wing center section. The 35R program ended in August, 1951 but some 35R c/n were not completed until 1952. All 13 35R were 1947 Model 35 Bonanzas:

35R - 1947 - 13 airplanes:
R-1 (D-25), R-2 (D-3), R-3 (D-721), R-4 (D-838), R-5 (D-588), R-6 (D-535), R-7 (D-532), R-9 (D-944), R-10 (D-1186), R-11 (D-92), R-12 (D-329), R-13 (D-418)

35	1948	D-1210 - D-1500 (except D-1424)	290
35R	1948	R-8 (D-1424)	1
A35	1949	D-1501 - D-2200, D-15001	701

NOTE: D-15001 was a production A35 built strictly for factory experimental work. The high c/n was intentionally chosen because regular production was never expected to reach that number.

MODEL	YEAR	CONSTRUCTOR NUMBER	TOTAL DELIVERED
B35	1950	D-2201 - D-2680	480
C35	1951	D-2681 - D-3090	410
C35	1952	D-3091 - D-3292, D-3294 - D-3400	309
D35	1953	D-3401 - D-3698	298
E35	1954	D-3699 - D-3998, D-3293	301
F35	1955	D-3999 - D-4375, D-4377 - D-4391	392
G35	1956	D-4392 - D-4865, D-4376, D-15002	476

NOTE: D-15002 was a production G35 built strictly for factory experimental work.

MODEL	YEAR	CONSTRUCTOR NUMBER	TOTAL DELIVERED
H35	1957	D-4866 - D-5061, D-5063 - D-5330	464
J35	1958	D-5331 - D-5725, D-5062	396
K35	1959	D-5726 - D-6161	436
M35	1960	D-6162 - D-6561	400
N35	1961	D-6562 - D-6841	280
O35	1961	Unknown	1

NOTE: The O35 was an experimental Bonanza equipped with a laminar flow wing and trailing beam-type main landing gear. Entire wing leading edge was a wet cell for increased fuel capacity. Engine was 260 hp IO-470N. No production O35 were built. It is included here strictly because of its alphabetical sequence with other Bonanzas.

MODEL	YEAR	CONSTRUCTOR NUMBER	TOTAL DELIVERED
P35	1962	D-6842 - D-7066	225
P35	1963	D-7067 - D-7139, D-7141 - D-7309	242
S35	1964	D-7310 - D-7639, D-7140	331
S35	1965	D-7640 - D-7967	328
S35	1966	D-7968 - D-7976	9
V35/V3 5TC	1966	D-7977 - D-8301	325

NOTE: The following list contains c/n for 1966 V35TC turbocharged models built concurrently with naturally-aspirated V35 airplanes:
V35TC - 1966 - 37 airplanes:

D-8036, D-8048, D-8057, D-8064, D-8072, D-8075, D-8090, D-8127, D-8133, D-8140, D-8146, D-8153, D-8176, D-8181, S-8184, D-8188, D-8190, D-8194, D-8199, D-8205, D-8210, D-8217, D-8225, D-8229, D-8234, D-8239, D-8242, D-8245, D-8249, D-8255, D-8261, D-8267, D-8274, D-8279, D-8286, D-8294, D-8300

MODEL	YEAR	CONSTRUCTOR NUMBER	TOTAL DELIVERED
V35	1967	D-8302 - D-8598	297

NOTE: The following list contains c/n for 1967 V35TC turbocharged models built concurrently with naturally-aspirated V35 airplanes:
V35TC - 1967 - 42 airplanes:

D-8307, D-8316, D-8323, D-8328, D-8336, D-8346, D-8353, D-8359, D-8366, D-8373, D-8379, D-8385, D-8393, D-8400, D-8407, D-8419, D-8427, D-8432, D-8438, D-8447, D-8456, D-8465, D-8470, D-8475, D-8481, D-8485, D-8490, D-8496, D-8500, D-8505, D-8509, D-8514, D-8518, D-8526, D-8530, D-8533, D-8540, D-8552, D-8560, D-8567, D-8577, D-8596

MODEL	YEAR	CONSTRUCTOR NUMBER	TOTAL DELIVERED
V35A/V35A-TC	1968	D-8599 - D-8871	273

NOTE: The following list contains c/n for 1968 V35A-TC turbocharged models built concurrently with naturally-aspirated V35A airplanes:
V35A-TC - 1968 - 26 airplanes:

D-8606, D-8615, D-8625, D-8628, D-8638, D-8652, D-8662, D-8673, D-8681, D-8694, D-8705, D-8715, D-8730, D-8744, D-8763, D-8777, D-8790, D-8810, D-8823, D-8829, D-8835, D-8842, D-8849, D-8855, D-8861, D-8868

MODEL	YEAR	CONSTRUCTOR NUMBER	TOTAL DELIVERED
V35A/V35A-TC	1969	D-8872 - D-9068	197

NOTE: The following list contains c/n for 1969 V35A-TC turbocharged models built concurrently with naturally-aspirated V35A airplanes:
V35A-TC - 1969 - 20 airplanes:
D-8875, D-8887, D-8901, D-8911, D-8921, D-8930, D-8940, D-8951, D-8961, D-8973, D-8982, D-8992, D-9001, D-9008, D-9019, D-9027, D-9039, D-9048, D-9055, D-9063, D-9070, D-9078, D-9088, D-9107, D-9131, D-9154, D-9180

MODEL	YEAR	CONSTRUCTOR NUMBER	TOTAL DELIVERED
V35B/V35B-TC	1970	D-9069 - D-9204, D-9207 - D-9211	141

NOTE: The following list contains c/n for 1970 V35B-TC turbocharged models built concurrently with naturally-aspirated V35B airplanes:
V35B-TC - 1970 - 7 airplanes:
D-9070, D-9078, D-9088, D-9107, D-9131, D-9154, D-9180

MODEL	YEAR	CONSTRUCTOR NUMBER	TOTAL DELIVERED
V35B	1971	D-9205, D-9206, D-9212 - D-9286	77
V35B	1972	D-9287 - D-9390	104
V35B	1973	D-9391 - D-9537	147
V35B	1974	D-9538 - D-9686	149
V35B	1975	D-9687 - D-9815	129
V35B	1976	D-9816 - D-9947	132
V35B	1977	D-9948 - D-10068	121
V35B	1978	D-10069 - D-10178	110
V35B	1979	D-10179 - D-10302	124
V35B	1980	D-10303 - D-10353	51
V35B	1981	D-10354 - D-10382	29
V35B	1982	D-10383 - D-10403*	21

*NOTE: D-10403 was last V-tail Bonanza built, delivered to production flight test on 11-2-82. Delivered in May, 1984. Last V-tail Bonanza delivered to a retail customer was D-10399, delivered in August, 1984.

Model 36 Series

MODEL	YEAR	CONSTRUCTOR NUMBER	TOTAL DELIVERED
36	1968	E-1 - E-105	105
36	1969	E-106 - E-184	79
A36	1970	E-185 - E-240	56
A36	1971	E-241 - E-282	42
A36	1972	E-283 - E-363	81
A36	1973	E-364 - E-476	113
A36	1974	E-477 - E-604	128
A36	1975	E-605 - E-765	161
A36	1976	E-766 - E-926	161
A36	1977	E-927 - E-1110, E-1112 - E-1151	224
A36	1978	E-1111, E-1152 - E-1370	224
A36	1979	E-1371 - E-1593	223
A36	1980	E-1594 - E-1765	172
A36	1981	E-1766 - E-1931	166
A36	1982	E-1932 - E-2049	117
A36	1983	E-2050 - E-2103, E-2105 - E-2110	59
A36	1984	E-2104, E-2111 - E-2204	95
A36	1985	E-2205 - E-2277, E-2279 - E-2289, E-2293 - E-2295	87
A36	1986	E-2278, E-2290, E-2291, E-2292, E-2296 - E-2352	60
A36	1987	E-2353 - E-2402	49
A36	1988	E-2403 - E-2467	65
A36	1989	E-2468 - E-2518	51
A36	1990	E-2519 - E-2586 (except E-2581)	67
A36	1991	E-2581, E-2587 - E-2686	101
A36	1992	E-2687	
A36TC	1979	EA-1 - EA-32	32
A36TC	1980	EA-33 - EA-158	126
A36TC	1981	EA-159 - EA-241, EA-243 - EA-272	113
B36TC	1981	EA-242	1
B36TC	1982	EA-273 - EA-319, EA-321 - EA-323	50
B36TC	1983	EA-324 - EA-388	65
B36TC	1984	EA-320, EA-389 - EA-442	54
B36TC	1985	EA-443 - EA-451	8
B36TC	1986	EA-452 - EA-461	9
B36TC	1987	EA-462 and after	
B36TC	1987	EA-462 - EA-473	12
B36TC	1988	EA-474 - EA-488	15
B36TC	1989	EA-489 - EA-500	12
B36TC	1990	EA-501 - EA-513	13
B36TC	1991	EA-514 - EA-528	15
B36TC	1992	EA-529	

Model 45 Series

NOTE: Early production Model B45, T-34A and T-34B are listed by deliveries in fiscal year, not calendar year. Beech built commercial and military versions of the Model 45 from 1950 to 1959. Constructor numbers are not presented for these airplanes:

MODEL	YEAR	CONSTRUCTOR NUMBER	TOTAL DELIVERED
A45T	1950	YT-34BH - U.S. Army	3
T-34A	1953-54	U.S. Air Force	88
B45	1953-54	Commercial deliveries	85
T-34A	1954-55	U.S. Air Force	122
T-34B	1954-55	U.S. Navy	45
B45	1954-55	Commercial deliveries	47
T-34A	1955-56	U.S. Air Force	138
T-34B	1955-56	U.S. Navy	219
B45	1955-56	Commercial deliveries	21
T-34B	1956-57	U.S. Navy	147
B45	1956-57	Commercial deliveries	45
T-34B	1957-58	U.S. Navy	12
B45	1957-58	Commercial deliveries	29
B45	1958-59	Commercial deliveries	91

NOTE: Fuji Heavy Industries built the T-34A under license for Japan's emerging Self-Defense Force in the 1950s. The Japanese built 137 T-34.

Model 45 Series - Turbine-powered

MODEL	YEAR	CONSTRUCTOR NUMBER	TOTAL DELIVERED
34C	1979	GP-1 - GP-6	6

NOTE: GP-1 - GP-6 originally designated GM-72 - GM-77.

(Refer to 1978 T-34C-1)

MODEL	YEAR	CONSTRUCTOR NUMBER	TOTAL DELIVERED
34C	1984	GP-7 - GP-15	8
34C	1985	GP-16 - GP-50	35
34C	1986	GP-51	1
T-34C	1976	GL-1, GL-2	2
T-34C	1977	GL-3 - GL-72	70
T-34C	1978	GL-73 - GL-138	66
T-34C	1979	GL-139 - GL-163	25
T-34C	1981	GL-164 - GL-184	21
T-34C	1983	GL-232 - GL-237, GL-241, GL-231, GL-238 - GL-240, GL-242 - GL-334	97

NOTE: GL-334 delivered to U.S. Navy 6-84. No T-34C were built in 1985-88.

MODEL	YEAR	CONSTRUCTOR NUMBER	TOTAL DELIVERED
T-34C	1989-90	GL-335 - GL-353	19
T-34C-1	1977	GM-2 - GM-10, GM-14 - GM-20	16

NOTE: GM-14 built as Beech factory demonstrator.

MODEL	YEAR	CONSTRUCTOR NUMBER	TOTAL DELIVERED
T-34C-1	1978	GM-11 - GM-13, GM-21 - GM-71	54

NOTE: GM-72 - GM-77 redesignated GP-1 - GP-6 in 1979. (Refer to 1979 Model 34C)

MODEL	YEAR	CONSTRUCTOR NUMBER	TOTAL DELIVERED
T-34C-1	1979	GM-78	1

NOTE: GM-78 built as Beech factory demonstrator.

MODEL	YEAR	CONSTRUCTOR NUMBER	TOTAL DELIVERED
T-34C-1	1980	GM-79-GM-81	3
T-34C-1	1981	GM-82 - GM-84	3
T-34C-1	1982	GM-85 - GM-88	3
T-34C-1	1983	GM-1, GM-89	2

NOTE: GM-1 originally built as Beech factory demonstrator in 1977. Sold and delivered in 1983.

MODEL	YEAR	CONSTRUCTOR NUMBER	TOTAL DELIVERED
T-34C-1	1984	GM-90 - GM-98	9

Model 50 Series

MODEL	YEAR	CONSTRUCTOR NUMBER	TOTAL DELIVERED
50	1952	H-1 - H-11	11
50 (YL-23)	1951	Military prototypes - L-23A series	4
B50	1953	CH-12 - CH-110	99
B50 (U-8D/L-23A)	1952	LH-9 (s/n 52-1801)	1
C50	1954	CH-111 - CH-135	25
C50	1955	CH-136 - CH-351	216
C50	1956	CH-352 - CH-360	9
D50	1956	DH-1 - DH-143	143

NOTE: DH-88 - DH-91 became L-23E.

MODEL	YEAR	CONSTRUCTOR NUMBER	TOTAL DELIVERED
D50	1956	DH-88 - DH-91 s/n 56-4039, 56-4041, s/n 56-4043, 56-4044	4
D50	1957	DH-144 - DH-154	11
D50A	1958	DH-155 - DH-198	44
D50B	1959	DH-199 - DH-236	38
D50C	1960	DH-237 - DH-300	64
D50E	1961	DH-301 - DH-325	25
D50E	1962	DH-326 - DH-333	8
D50E	1963	DH-334 - DH-347	14
E50	1957	EH-1 - EH-70	70
E50 (U-8D)	1957	LH-96 - LH-151 s/n 56-3695 - 56-3718 s/n 57-3084 - 57-3101 s/n 57-6077 - 57-6090	56
E50 (RU-8D)	1957	RLH-1 - RLH-8 s/n 57-6029 - 57-6036	8
E50 (RU-8D)	1958	LH-152 - LH-180 s/n 57-6091 - 57-6094 s/n 58-1329 - 583059	29
E50 (RU-8D)	1958	RLH-9 - RLH-48 s/n 57-6037 - 57-6076 RLH-49 - RLH-60 s/n 58-3048 - 58-3059	52
E50 (RU-8D)	1959	LHC-3 - LHC-10 s/n 58-1357 - 58-1364 LH-192 - LH-195 s/n 59-2535 - 59-2538	12
E50 (RU-8D)	1959	RLH-61 - RLH-93 s/n 58-3060 - 58-3092	33
E50 (U-8G)	1960	LHE-6 - LHE-16 s/n 56-3710, 58-3060 s/n 58-3092, 58-1332 s/n 58-3057, 58-3059 s/n 58-3093, 58-3062 s/n 58-1331, 58-3055 s/n 58-1336	11
F50	1958	FH-71 - FH-93, FH-95, FH-96,	25
G50	1959	GH-94, GH-97 - GH-119	24

NOTE: FH-94 redesignated GH-94.

MODEL	YEAR	CONSTRUCTOR NUMBER	TOTAL DELIVERED
H50	1960	HH-120 - HH-149	30
J50	1961	JH-150 - JH-161	12
J50	1962	JH-162 - JH-170	9
J50	1963	JH-171 - JH-176	6

NOTE: Model 50 series designated "Twin Bonanza".

Model 95-55 - Model 55 Series

MODEL	YEAR	CONSTRUCTOR NUMBER	TOTAL DELIVERED
95-55	1961	TC-1 - TC-190	190
95-A55	1962	TC-191 - TC-349, TC-351 - TC-370, TC-372 - TC-379	187
95-A55	1963	TC-380 - TC-501	122
95-B55	1964	TC-371, TC-502 - TC-771	271
95-B55	1965	TC-772 - TC-965	194
B55B (T-42A)	1965	TF-1 - TF-25 s/n 65-12679 - 65-12703	25
95-B55	1966	TC-966 - TC-1016	51

MODEL	YEAR	CONSTRUCTOR NUMBER	TOTAL DELIVERED
B55B (T-42A)	1966	TF-26 - TF-65 s/n 65-12704 - 65-12733 s/n 66-4300 - 66-4309	40
95-C55	1966	TC-350	1
95-C55	1966	TE-1 - TE-49, TE-51 - TE-266	265
95-B55	1967	TC-1017 - TC-1042	26
95-C55	1967	TE-267 - TE-451	185
95-B55	1968	TC-1043 - TC-1156	114
D55	1968	TE-452 - TE-632	181
95-B55	1969	TC-1157 - TC-1287	131
D55	1969	TE-633 - TE-767	135
95-B55	1970	TC-1288 - TC-1365, TC-1367, TC-1369 - TC-1371	81
E55	1970	TE-768 - TE-824, TE-826, TE-827	59
95-B55	1971	TC-1366, TC-1368, TC-1370, TC-1372 - TC-1401	
B55B (T-42A)	1971	TF-66 - TF-70 s/n 71-21053 - 71-21057	5

NOTE: TF-66 - TF-70 foreign sales. Affected c/n were: TC-1393 (TF-66), TC-1394 (TF-67), TC-1395 (TF-68), TC-1396 (TF-69), TC-1402 (TF-70).

MODEL	YEAR	CONSTRUCTOR NUMBER	TOTAL DELIVERED
E55	1971	TE-825, TE-828 - TE-846	20
95-B55	1972	TC-1403 - TC-1484	82
E55	1972	TE-847 - TE-879	33
95-B55	1973	TC-1485 - TC-1607	123
E55	1973	TE-880 - TE-937, TE-939 - TE-942	62
95-B55	1974	TC-1608 - TC-1781	174
E55	1974	TE-938, TE-943 - TE-1001	60
95-B55	1975	TC-1782 - TC-1905	124
E55	1975	TE-1002 - TE-1064	63
95-B55	1976	TC-1906 - TC-2002	97
E55	1976	TE-1065 - TE-1083	19
95-B55	1977	TC-2003 - TC-2091	89
E55	1977	TE-1084 - TE-1113	30
95-B55	1978	TC-2092 - TC-2180	89
E55	1978	TE-1114 - TE-1142	29
95-B55	1979	TC-2181 - TC-2275	95
E55	1979	TE-1143 - TE-1168	26
95-B55	1980	TC-2276 - TC-2354	79
E55	1980	TE-1169 - TE-1182	14
95-B55	1981	TC-2355 - TC-2420	66
E55	1981	TE-1183 - TE-1195	13
95-B55	1982	TC-2421 - TC-2456	36
E55	1982	TE-1196 - TE-1201	6

NOTE: Model 55 series designated "Baron".

Model 56 Series

MODEL	YEAR	CONSTRUCTOR NUMBER	TOTAL DELIVERED
56TC	1967	TG-2 - TG-51	50
56TC	1968	TG-52 - TG-71	20
56TC	1969	TG-72 - TG-83	12
A56TC	1970	TG-84 - TG-92	9
A56TC	1971	TG-93 - TG-94	2

NOTE: Model 56TC designated "Turbo Baron".

Model 58 Series

MODEL	YEAR	CONSTRUCTOR NUMBER	TOTAL DELIVERED
58	1969	TH-1	1
58	1970	TH-2 - TH-94, TH-96 - TH-98, TH-101 - TH-102	98
58	1971	TH-95, TH-99, TH-100, TH-103 - TH-174	75
58	1972	TH-175 - TH-263	89
58	1973	TH-264 - TH-384	121
58	1974	TH-385 - TH-524	140
58	1975	TH-525 - TH-679	155
58	1976	TH-680 - TH-772	93
58	1977	TH-773 - TH-872	100
58	1978	TH-873 - TH-972	100
58	1979	TH-973 - TH-1079	107
58	1980	TH-1080 - TH-1193	114
58	1981	TH-1194 - TH-1297	104
58	1982	TH-1298 - TH-1355	58
58	1983	TH-1356 - TH-1388, TH-1390 - TH-1395	40
58	1984	TH-1389, TH-1396 - TH-1435	41
58	1985	TH-1436 - TH-1504*	69
58	1987	TH-1508 - TH-1531	24
58	1988	TH-1532 - TH-1544	13
58	1989	TH-1545 - TH-1575	31
58	1990	TH-1576 - TH-1612	37
58	1991	TH-1613 - TH-1648	36
58	1992	TH-1649	

*NOTE: The following 1985 Model 58 were converted to 1986 models: TH-1439, TH-1444, TH-1449, TH-1453 - TH-1455, TH-1460, TH-1465, TH-1470, TH-1475, TH-1476, TH-1486, TH-1487, TH-1489 - TH-1491, TH-1494, TH-1498, TH-1501, TH-1503, TH-1505, TH-1506, TH-1507 58 1987 TH-1508 and after

NOTE: Model 58 designated "Baron".

Model 58P Series

MODEL	YEAR	CONSTRUCTOR NUMBER	TOTAL DELIVERED
58P	1976	TJ-3 - TJ-85	83
58P	1977	TJ-86 - TJ-122	37
58P	1978	TJ-123 - TJ-168	46
58P	1979	TJ-169 - TJ-209, TJ-211 - TJ-234	65
58P	1980	TJ-210, TJ-235 - TJ-316	83
58P	1981	TJ-317 - TJ-384	68
58P	1982	TJ-385 - TJ-431	47
58P	1983	TJ-432 - TJ-435, TJ-437 - TJ-443	11
58P	1984	TJ-436, TJ-444 - TJ-470	28
58P	1985	TJ-471 - TJ-497	27
58P	1986-1991		Not Built

NOTE: Model 58P designated "Pressurized Baron".

Model 58TC Series

MODEL	YEAR	CONSTRUCTOR NUMBER	TOTAL DELIVERED
58TC	1976	TK-1 - TK-34	34
58TC	1977	TK-35 - TK-60	26
58TC	1978	TK-61 - TK-84	24
58TC	1979	TK-85 - TK-109	25
58TC	1980	TK-110 - TK-133	24
58TC	1981	TK-134 - TK-145	12
58TC	1982	TK-146 - TK-149	4
58TC	1983	TK-150	1
58TC	1984	TK-151	1
58TC	1985-1991		Not Built

NOTE: Model 58TC designated "Baron".

Model 60 Series

MODEL	YEAR	CONSTRUCTOR NUMBER	TOTAL DELIVERED
60	1968	P-4 - P-18	15
60	1969	P-19 - P-109	91
60	1970	P-110 - P-122, P-124, P-125, P-126	16
A60	1970	P-123, P-127 - P-139, P-141 - P-146, P-148, P-149, P-151	23
A60	1971	P-140, P-147, P-150, P-152 - P-162, P-167 - P-175, P-178 - P-180, P-182	27
A60	1972	P-163 - P-166, P-176, P-177, P-181, P-183 - P-202, P-210	28
A60	1973	P-203 - P-209, P-211 - P-246	43
B60	1974	P-247 - P-307	61
B60	1975	P-308 - P-347, P-349 - P-364	56
B60	1976	P-348, P-365 - P-401	38
B60	1977	P-402 - P-445	44
B60	1978	P-446 - P-485	40
B60	1979	P-486 - P-510, P-512 - P-519	33
B60	1980	P-511, P-520 - P-555	37
B60	1981	P-556 - P-580	25
B60	1982	P-581 - P-596	16

NOTE: Model 60 series designated "Duke".

Model 65 Series

MODEL	YEAR	CONSTRUCTOR NUMBER	TOTAL DELIVERED
65 (U-8F)	1959	L-3 - L-5 s/n 58-1354 - 58-1356	3

MODEL	YEAR	CONSTRUCTOR NUMBER	TOTAL DELIVERED
65	1960	L-1, L-2, L-6, LF-7, LF-8, LC-1 - LC-52	56
65 (U-8F)	1960	LF-8 - LF-24 s/n 66-15365, 60-3453 - 60-3463, 60-5386 - 60-5390	17
65	1961	LC-53 - LC-112	60
65 (U-8F)	1961	LF-25 - LF-29 s/n 61-2426 - 61-2430	5
65	1962	LC-113 - LC-147	35
65 (U-8F)	1962	LF-30 - LF-74 s/n 61-3832 - 62-3875, 63-7975	45
65	1963	LC-148 - LC-156	9
65 (U-8F)	1963	LF-75, LF-76 s/n 63-13636, 63-13637	2
65	1964	LC-157 - LC-159	3
65	1965	LC-160 - LC-192	33
65	1966	LC-193 - LC-237	45
65	1967	LC-238, LC-239	2
A65	1967	LC-240 - LC-268	29
A65	1968	LC-269 - LC-272	4
A65-8200*	1968	LC-273 - LC-306	34
A65-8200*	1969	LC-307 - LC-324	18
A65	1969	LC-325 - LC-329	5
A65	1970	LC-330 - LC-335	6

NOTE: Model 65 series designated "Queen Air". *A65-8200 approved for 8,200-pound gross weight.

Model 70 Series

MODEL	YEAR	CONSTRUCTOR NUMBER	TOTAL DELIVERED
70	1969	LB-1 - LB-20	20
70	1970	LB-21 - LB-34	14
70	1971	LB-35	1

NOTE: Model 70 series designated "Queen Air".

Model 73

MODEL	YEAR	CONSTRUCTOR NUMBER	TOTAL DELIVERED
73	1955	Experimental	1

NOTE: Model 73 "Jet Mentor" was Beech prototype for USAF/U.S. Navy jet trainer competition. Only one built.

Model 76 Series

MODEL	YEAR	CONSTRUCTOR NUMBER	TOTAL DELIVERED
76	1978	ME-1 - ME-72	72
76	1979	ME-73 - ME-282, ME-284 - ME-286	213
76	1980	ME-283, ME-287 - ME-371	86
76	1981	ME-372 - ME-426	55
76	1982	ME-427 - ME-437	11

NOTE: Model 76 designated "Duchess".

Model 77 Series

MODEL	YEAR	CONSTRUCTOR NUMBER	TOTAL DELIVERED
77	1979	WA-1 - WA-47	47
77	1980	WA-48 - WA-187	140
77	1981	WA-188 - WA-312	125

NOTE: Model 77 designated "Skipper".

Model 65-80, 65-A80, 65-B80 Series

MODEL	YEAR	CONSTRUCTOR NUMBER	TOTAL DELIVERED
65-80	1962	LD-1 - LD-33, LD-35 - LD-45, LD-47 - LD-55	53
65-80	1963	LD-56 - LD-150	95
65-A80*	1964	LD-34, LD-46, LD-151 - LD-193	45
65-A80*	1965	LD-194 - LD-249	56
65-A80*	1966	LD-250 - LD-269	20

NOTE: 65-A80 series designated "Queen Air". *A65-A80 approved for 8,800-pound gross weight.

MODEL	YEAR	CONSTRUCTOR NUMBER	TOTAL DELIVERED
65-B80	1966	LD-270 - LD-313	44
65-B80	1967	LD-314 - LD-361	48
65-B80	1968	LD-362 - LD-405	44
65-B80	1969	LD-406 - LD-425	20
65-B80	1970	LD-426 - LD-433, LD-437, LD-439, LD-441	11
65-B80	1971	LD-434, LD-435, LD-436, LD-438, LD-440, LD-442 - LD-447	11
65-B80	1972	LD-448 - LD-460	13
65-B80	1973	LD-461 - LD-472	12
65-B80	1974	LD-473 - LD-487	15
65-B80	1975	LD-488 - LD-505	18
65-B80	1976	LD-506, LD-507	2
65-B80	1977	LD-508 - LD-511	4

NOTE: Model 65-B80 designated "Queen Air".

Model 87

MODEL	YEAR	CONSTRUCTOR NUMBER	TOTAL DELIVERED
87 (NU-8F)	1963	LG-1 s/n 63-12902	1

NOTE: Prototype for U-21 series, designated YU-21.

Model 65-88 Series

MODEL	YEAR	CONSTRUCTOR NUMBER	TOTAL DELIVERED
65-88	1965	LP-1 - LP-4	4
65-88	1966	LP-5 - LP-26, LP-28, LP-30 - LP-40	34

NOTE: LP-27 converted to LJ-178A, LP-29 converted to LJ-116. Both airplanes equipped with PT6A-6 turboprop engine installation similar to Model 65-90 King Air.

MODEL	YEAR	CONSTRUCTOR NUMBER	TOTAL DELIVERED
65-88	1967	LP-41 - LP-45	5
65-88	1968	LP-46	1
65-88	1969	LP-47	1

NOTE: 65-88 series originally designated Model 85, but were produced as Model 65-88 Queen Air. It was the first production piston-engine Beechcraft to feature a pressurized cabin.

Model 65-90 Series

MODEL	YEAR	CONSTRUCTOR NUMBER	TOTAL DELIVERED
65-90	1964	LJ-1 - LJ-7	7
65-90	1965	LJ-8 - LJ-75, LJ-77	69
65-90	1966	LJ-78-LJ-113	36
65-A90	1966	LJ-114 - LJ-183, LJ-76, LJ-178A	72
65-A90	1967	LJ-184 - LJ-317	134

NOTE: 65-90 - 65-A90 series designated "King Air".

MODEL	YEAR	CONSTRUCTOR NUMBER	TOTAL DELIVERED
A90-1 (U-21A)	1967	LM-1 - LM-77 s/n 66-18000 - 67-18076 LM-78 - LM-84 s/n 67-18078 - 67-18084 LM-85, LM-86 s/n 67-18086 - 67-18088 LM-87 - LM-89 s/n 67-18090 - 67-18092 LM-90, LM-91 s/n 67-18094 - 67-18095	91
A90-2 (RU-21B)	1967	LS-1 - LS-3 s/n 67-18077, 67-18087 67-18093	3
A90-3 (RU-21C)	1967	LT-1, LT-2 s/n 67-18085, 67-18089	2
A90-1 (U-21A)	1968	LM-92 - LM-99 s/n 67-18096 - 67-18103 LM-115 - LM-117 s/n 67-18116 - 67-18118	11
A90-1 (RU-21A)	1968	LM-108 - LM-111 s/n 67-18112 - 67-18115	4

MODEL	YEAR	CONSTRUCTOR NUMBER	TOTAL DELIVERED
A90-1 (RU-21D)	1968	LM-100 - LM-107 s/n 67-18104 - 67-18111 LM-115 - LM-117 s/n 67-18119 - 67-18121	10
A90-1 (RU-21D)	1969	LM-118 - LM-124 s/n 67-18122 - 67-18128	7
A90-1 (U-21G)	1971	LM-125 - LM-141 s/n 70-15891 - 70-15907	17
A90-4 (RU-21E) (RU-21H)	1971	LU-1 - LU-16 s/n 70-15875 - 70-15890	16

Model B90 Series

Model	Year	CN	Total
B90	1968	LJ-318 - LJ-408	91
B90	1969	LJ-409 - LJ-481	73
B90	1970	LJ-482 - LJ-501	20

NOTE: Model B90 series designated "King Air".

Model C90 Series

Model	Year	CN	Total
C90	1971	LJ-502 - LJ-533	32
C90	1972	LJ-534 - LJ-567	34
C90	1973	LJ-568 - LJ-608	41
C90	1974	LJ-609 - LJ-641	33
C90	1975	LJ-642 - LJ-673	32
C90	1976	LJ-674 - LJ-701	28
C90	1977	LJ-702 - LJ-741	40
C90	1978	LJ-742 - LJ-802	61
C90	1979	LJ-803 - LJ-869	67
C90	1980	LJ-870 - LJ-925	56
C90	1981	LJ-926 - LJ-985, LJ-987 - LJ-993	67
C90	1982	LJ-994, LJ-995, LJ-997 - LJ-1010	16
C90-1	1982	LJ-986, LJ-996, LJ-1011 - LJ-1044, LJ-1047	37
C90-1	1983	LJ-1045, LJ-1046, LJ-1048 - LJ-1062	17
C90A	1984	LJ-1063 - LJ-1084, LJ-1086 - LJ-1087	24
C90A	1985	LJ-1085, LJ-1088 - LJ-1127	41
C90A	1986	LJ-1128 - LJ-1137	9
C90A	1987	LJ-1138 and after*	
C90A	1987	LJ-1138, LJ-142 - LJ-1163	23
C90A	1988	LJ-1164 - LJ-1190	27
C90A	1989	LJ-1191 - LJ-1227	37
C90A	1990	LJ-1228 - LJ-1269	42
C90A	1991	LJ-1270 - LJ-1296	26
C90A	1992	LJ-1297, LJ-1298, LJ-1299 (LJ-1299 ends C90A production)	3
C90B	1992	LJ-1288, LJ-1295, LJ-1300	

*NOTE: LJ-1138 is prototype for C90A with gross weight increase.

NOTE: Model C90 series designated "King Air".

Model E90 Series

Model	Year	CN	Total
E90	1972	LW-1 - LW-16, LW-18 - LW-23	22
E90	1973	LW-17, LW-24 - LW-73	51
E90	1974	LW-74 - LW-117	44
E90	1975	LW-118 - LW-156	39
E90	1976	LW-157 - LW-201	45
E90	1977	LW-202 - LW-251	50
E90	1978	LW-252 - LW-301	50
E90	1979	LW-302 - LW-327	26
E90	1980	LW-328 - LW-341	14
E90	1981	LW-342 - LW-347	6

NOTE: Model E90 designated "King Air".

Model F90 Series

Model	Year	CN	Total
F90	1979	LA-2 - LA-8	7

NOTE: LA-1 converted to LE-0 for experimental work.

Model	Year	CN	Total
F90	1980	LA-9 - LA-81	73
F90	1981	LA-82 - LA-156	75
F90	1982	LA-157 - LA-183, LA-185 - LA-197, LA-199	41
F90	1983	LA-184, LA-198, LA-200, LA-201, LA-203, LA-204	6
F90-1	1983	LA-202, LA-205 - LA-214	11
F90-1	1984	LA-215 - LA-225	11
F90-1	1985	LA-226 - LA-236	11
F90-1	1986	LA-237	1

NOTE: F90 - F90-1 series designated "King Air".

Model H90

NOTE: Model H90 was produced for the U.S. Navy with military designation T-44A, not equivalent to any King Air. None were built for commercial sale. The c/n and military serial number are presented:

Model	Year	CN	Total
H90	1977	LL-1 - LL-13 s/n 160839 - 160851	13
H90	1978	LL-14 - LL-35 s/n 160852 - 160856, s/n 160967 - 160983	21
H90	1979	LL-36 - LL-58 s/n 160984 - 160986, s/n 161057 - 161076	23
H90	1980	LL-59 - LL-61 s/n 161077 - 161079	3

Model 95 Series

Model	Year	CN	Total
95	1958	TD-2 - TD-173, TD-185	173
95	1959	TD-174 - TD-184, TD-186 - TD-302	128
B95	1960	TD-303 - TD-452	150
B95A	1961	TD-453 - TD-491	39
B95A	1962	TD-492 - TD-533	42
D95A	1963	TD-534 - TD-552	19
D95A	1964	TD-553 - TD-592	40
D95A	1965	TD-593 - TD-640	48
D95A	1966	TD-641 - TD-673	33
D95A	1967	TD-674 - TD-707	34
E95	1968	TD-708 - TD-721	14

NOTE: Model 95 series designated "Travel Air".

Model 99 Series

Model	Year	CN	Total
99	1968	U-1 - U-35, U-37 - U-45	44
99A	1968	U-36	1

NOTE: U-36 was Beech factory demonstrator. Sold 9-30-71.

Model	Year	CN	Total
99	1969	U-46 - U-49, U-51 - U-79, U-86 - U-88, U-90 - U-92, U-94, U-95, U-98, U-99, U-100, U-102, U-103, U-106 - U-109, U-114, U-119 - U-122, U-124	56

NOTE: U-50 was Model 99, became prototype C99 in 1980.

Model	Year	CN	Total
99A	1969	U-80 - U-85, U-89, U-93, U-96, U-97, U-101, U-104, U-105, U-110 - U-113, U-115 - U-118, U-123, U-125 - U-127	25

MODEL	YEAR	CONSTRUCTOR NUMBER	TOTAL DELIVERED
99	1970	U-136	1
99A	1970	U-128 - U-131, U-133 - U-135, U-137 - U-145	16
A99A	1970	U-132	1
99A	1971	U-147	1
B99	1972	U-146, U-148, U-150, U-151	4

NOTE: U-148 sold 11-24-71 as 99A. Modifed to B99 7-14-72 at Beech factory.

MODEL	YEAR	CONSTRUCTOR NUMBER	TOTAL DELIVERED
B99	1973	U-149	1
B99	1974	U-152 - U-159	8
B99	1975	U-160 - U-164	5
C99	1982	U-50, U-165 - U-203	40
C99	1983	U-204 - U-216	13
C99	1984	U-217 - U-227	11
C99	1985	U-228 - U-233	6
C99	1986	U-234 - U-239	6
C99	1987	U-240 and after	
C99	1988-1991		Not Built

NOTE: Model 99 series designated "Airliner".

Model 100 - A100 - B100 Series

MODEL	YEAR	CONSTRUCTOR NUMBER	TOTAL DELIVERED
100	1969	B-2 - B-8	7

NOTE: B-1 was originally a Model 100, changed to Model A100 in fiscal year 1976.

MODEL	YEAR	CONSTRUCTOR NUMBER	TOTAL DELIVERED
100	1970	B-9 - B-65, B-68, B-70 B-72	60
100	1971	B-66, B-67, B-69, B-71, B-73 - B-89, B-93	22
A100	1972	B-90, B-91, B-92, B-94 - B-135, B-137, B-138	47
A100 (U-21F)	1971	B-95 - B-99 s/n 70-15908 - 70-15912	5
A100	1973	B-136, B-139 - B-177	40
A100	1974	B-178 - B-204	27
A100	1975	B-206 - B-222	17

NOTE: B-205 became Model B100 prototype BE-1.

MODEL	YEAR	CONSTRUCTOR NUMBER	TOTAL DELIVERED
A100	1976	B-1, B-223 - B-230	9
A100	1977	B-231 - B237	7
A100	1978	B-238 - B-240, B-242	4
A100	1979	B-241, B-243 - B-247	6
B100	1976	BE-1 - BE-16	16
B100	1977	BE-17 - BE-31	15
B100	1978	BE-32 - BE-54	23
B100	1979	BE-55 - BE-77	23
B100	1980	BE-78 - BE-102	25
B100	1981	BE-103 - BE-122	20
B100	1982	BE-123 - BE-132, BE-135	11
B100	1983	BE-133, BE-134, BE-136, BE-137	4

Model 200 - B200 Series

MODEL	YEAR	CONSTRUCTOR NUMBER	TOTAL DELIVERED
A100-1 (RU-21J) (U.S. Army)	1972	BB-3 - BB-5 s/n 71-21058 - 71-21060	3
200	1974	BB-2 - BB-17	13

NOTE: BB-1 was engineering prototype. BB-2 was Beech factory demonstrator.

MODEL	YEAR	CONSTRUCTOR NUMBER	TOTAL DELIVERED
200	1975	BB-18 - BB-88	71
A200 (C12A) (U.S. Army)	1975	BC-1 - BC-8 s/n 73-22250 - 73-22257 BC-9 - BC-10 s/n 73-22261, 73-22262	20
(U.S. Air Force)		BD-1 - BD-10 s/n 73-1205 - 73-1214	
200	1976	BB-89 - BB-185 BB-187, BB-188	99

NOTE: BB-186 became BT-1 with wing tip tanks in 1976.

MODEL	YEAR	CONSTRUCTOR NUMBER	TOTAL DELIVERED
A200 (C-12A) (U.S. Army)	1976	BC-11 - BC-13 s/n 73-22263 - 73-22265 BC-14 - BC-16 s/n 73-22258 - 73-22260 BC-17 - BC-2 s/n 73-22266 - 73-22269 BC-21, BC-22 s/n 76-22245 - 76-22246	32
(U.S. Air Force)		BD-11 - BD-14 s/n 73-1215 - 73-1218 BD-15 - BD-26 s/n 76-0158 - 76-0169 BD-27 - BD-30 s/n 76-0173, 76-0171, 76-0172, 76-0170	
200	1977	BB-189 - BB-202, BB-204 - BB-269, BB-271 - BB-300	110
A200 (C-12A) (U.S. Army)	1977	BC-23 - BC-33 s/n 76-22547 - 76-22557 BC-34, BC-35 - BC-41 s/n 76-22951, 76-22558 - 76-22564	19
200	1978	BB-301 - BB-407 BB-409 - BB-414	113
A200 (C-12A) (U.S. Army)	1978	BC-42 - BC-61 s/n 77-22931 - 77-22950	20
200	1979	BB-415 - BB-468, BB-470 - BB-488, BB-490 - BB-509, BB-511 - BB-529, BB-531 - BB-550, BB-552 - BB-562, BB-564 - BB-572	152
A200 (C-12C) (U.S. Army)	1979	BC-62 - BC-75 s/n 78-23126 - 78-23139	14
A200C (UC-12B) (U.S. Navy)	1979	BJ-1 - BJ-9 s/n 16-1185 - 16-1193	9
200	1980	BB-574 - BB-590, BB-592 - BB-608, BB-610 - BB-626, BB-628 - BB-646, B-648 - BB-664, BB-666 - BB-694, BB-696 - BB-733, BB-735 - BB-747	149
A200C (UC-12B) (U.S. Navy)	1980	BJ-10 - BJ-36 s/n 16-1194 - 16-1206 16-1306 - 16-1319	27
A200CT (C-12D) (U.S. Army)	1980	BP-1 - BP-6 s/n 78-23140 - 78-23145	6
200	1981	BB-734, BB-748 - BB-792, BB-794 - BB-797, BB-799 - BB-822, BB-824 - BB-828, BB-830 - BB-853, BB-872, BB-873, BB-892, BB-893, BB-912	108
A200C (UC-12B) (U.S. Navy)	1981	BJ-37 - BJ-58 s/n 16-1320 - 16-1327, 16-1497 - 16-1510	22
A200CT (C-12D) (U.S. Army)	1981	BP-7 - BP-11 BP-12 - BP-21 s/n 80-23371 - 80-23380	15

NOTE: BP-7 - BP-11 foreign sales.

MODEL	YEAR	CONSTRUCTOR NUMBER	TOTAL DELIVERED
B200	1981	BB-793, BB-829, BB-854 - BB-870, BB-874 - BB-891, BB-894, BB-896 - BB-911, BB-913 - BB-923, BB-925- BB-942*	83

*NOTE: BB-870 built as BL-36 with PT6A-41 engines. BB-871 built as BT-20 with PT6A-41 engines. BB-872 and BB-873 built with PT6A-41 engines. BB-892 and BB-893 built with PT6A-41 engines. BB-895 built as BT-21 with PT6A-41 engines. BB-912 built with PT6A-41 engines.

MODEL	YEAR	CONSTRUCTOR NUMBER	TOTAL DELIVERED
B200	1982	BB-924, BB-943 - BB-990, BB-992 - BB-1050, BB-1053 - BB-1090	147
A200C (UC-12B) (U.S. Navy)	1982	BJ-59 - BJ-66 s/n 16-1511 - 16-1518	8
A200C (UC-12F) (U.S. Navy)	1986	BU-1 - BU-12	12

NOTE: BU-11 and BU-12 modified by Beech for "RANSAC" firing range surveillance duty.

MODEL	YEAR	CONSTRUCTOR NUMBER	TOTAL DELIVERED
A200C (UC-12M) (U.S. Navy)	1987-88	BV-1 - BV-12	12
A200CT (C-12D) (U.S. Army)	1982	BP-22 - BP-27 s/n 81-23541 - 81-23546	6
B200	1983	BB-1051, BB-1091, BB-1092, BB-1094, BB-1095, BB-1099 - BB-1104, BB-1106 - BB-1116, BB-1118 - BB-1152, BB-1154 - BB-1156, BB-1159 - BB-1166	63
A200CT (C-12D) (U.S. Army)	1983	BP-28 - BP-34 s/n 82-23780 - 82-23785, 83-24145	7
A200CT (RC-12D) (U.S. Army)	1983	GR-1, GR-3 s/n 81-23542, 80-23377	2
B200	1984	BB-1153, BB-1157, BB-1168 - BB-1192	27
B200C (C-12F) (U.S. Air Force)	1984	BL-73 - BL-112 s/n 84-0143 - 84-0182	38
A200CT (C-12D) (U.S. Army)	1984	BP-35 - BP-39 s/n 83-24146 - 83-24150 BP-40 - BP-45 s/n 83-0494 - 83-0499	11
A200CT (C-12F) (U.S. Army)	1986	BP-51 - BP-69	19
A200CT (RC-12D) (U.S. Army)	1984	GR-2, GR-4 - GR-13 s/n 80-23371, 80-23373, 80-23375, 78-23141 - 78-23145, 80-23376, 80-23374, 80-23378	11
A200CT (U.S. Army)	1986-87	GR-14 - GR-19	6
A200CT (RC-12D) (U.S. Army)	1984	FC-1 - FC-3 s/n 80-23379, 80-23380, 80-23372	3
A200CT (RC-12K) (U.S. Army)	1986-87	FE-1 - FE-9	9
B200	1985	BB-1158, BB-1167, BB-1193 - BB-1242	52
B200	1986	BB-1243 - BB-1260	17
B200	1987	BB-1261 - BB-1286 (BB-1264 built as BT-31)	26
B200	1988	BB-1287 - BB-1315 (BB-1289, BB-1301 built as BT-32, BT-33; BB-1296, BB-1302, BB-1305, BB-1309, BB-1314 built as Model 1300)	29
B200	1989	BB-1316 - BB-1348 (BB-1338, BB-1339, BB-1340, BB-1341, BB-1342, BB-1343 built as Model 1300)	33

MODEL	YEAR	CONSTRUCTOR NUMBER	TOTAL DELIVERED
B200	1990	BB-1349 - BB-1391 (BB-1376, BB-1383, BB-1384 built as Model 1300)	43
B200	1991	BB-1392 - BB-1414	23
B200	1992	BB-1415 (BB-1426 built as BT-34)	

NOTE: Model 200 - B200 series designated "Super King Air".

Model 200C - B200C Series

NOTE: Model 200C and B200C equipped with cargo door.

MODEL	YEAR	CONSTRUCTOR NUMBER	TOTAL DELIVERED
200C	1979	BL-1 - BL-4	4
200C	1980	BL-5 - BL-13	9
200C	1981	BL-14 - BL-23, BL-25 - BL-36	22
B200C	1981	BL-37 - BL-43	7
B200C	1982	BL-44 - BL-57	14
B200C	1983	BL-61 - BL-71	11
B200C (C-12F) (U.S. Air Force)	1984	BL-72 - BL-123*	47

*NOTE: BL-73 - BL-112 assigned as C-12F for U.S. Air Force OSA program. BL-113 - BL-117 were not built. Six additional C-12F were built for Air National Guard units and assigned c/n BL-118 - BL-123. BL-73 - BL-112 delivered under lease, converted to sales in 12-86.

MODEL	YEAR	CONSTRUCTOR NUMBER	TOTAL DELIVERED
C-12F (U.S. Army)	1987-1988	BP-64 - BP-69	6
C-12F (U.S. Army)	1990	BP-70 & BP-71	2
FWC-12D (Foreign Military Sales to Israel)	1983	BP-7 - BP-11	5
UC-12M (U.S. Navy)	1987	BV-1 & BV-2	2
UC-12M (U.S. Navy)	1988	BV-2, BV-3 - BV-12	10
RC-12M (U.S. Navy)	1988	BV-11 & BV-12 Modified to RC-12M (U.S. Navy)	2
RC-12H (U.S. Army)	1986	GR-14, GR-17, GR-18	3
RC-12H (U.S. Army)	1987	GR-15, GR-16, GR-19	3
RC-12K (U.S. Army)	1988	FE-2, FE-4 - FE-9	7
RC-12K (U.S. Army)	1989	FE-1 & FE-3	2
RC-12K (U.S. Army)	1992	FE-10 - FE-19	10
RC-12K (U.S. Army)	1993	FE-20 - FE-25	6
RC-12K (U.S. Army)	1994	FE-26 - FE-31	6
B200C	1985	BL-124 - BL-126	3
B200C	1986	BL-127	1
B200C	1987	BL-128, BL-129	2
B200C	1988	BL-130 - BL-132	3
B200C	1989	BL-133 - BL-135	3
B200C	1990	BL-136 - BL-137	2
B200C	1991	Not built	
B200C	1992	BL-138	

Model 200T/200CT - B200T/B200CT Series

NOTE: Model 200CT and B200CT equipped with cargo door and wing tip tanks. Numbers in parentheses indicate original c/n before reassignment as 200CT and B200CT:

MODEL	YEAR	CONSTRUCTOR NUMBER	TOTAL DELIVERED
200CT	1981	BN-1 (BL-24)	1
B200CT	1982	BN-2 (BL-58)	1
B200CT	1983	BN-3 (BL-59), BN-4 (BL-60)	2

Model 200T - B200T Series

NOTE: Model 200T and B200T equipped with wing tip tanks.

MODEL	YEAR	CONSTRUCTOR NUMBER	TOTAL DELIVERED
200T	1976	BT-1 (BB-186)	1
200T	1977	BT-2 (BB-203), BT-3 (BB-270)	2
200T	1978	BT-4 (BB-408)	1
200T	1979	BT-5 (BB-469), BT-6 (BB-489), BT-7 (BB-510), BT-8 (BB-530), BT-9 (BB-551), BT-10 (BB-563), BT-11 (BB-573)	7
200T	1980	BT-12 (BB-591), BT-13 (BB-609), BT-14 (BB-627), BT-15 (BB-647), BT-16 (BB-665), BT-17 (BB-687), BT-18 (BB-695)	10
200T	1981	BT-19 (BB-823), BT-20 (BB-871), BT-21 (BB-895)	3
200T	1982	BT-22 (BB-991)	1
200T	1983	BT-28 (BB-1117)	1
B200T	1982	BT-23 (BB-1052)	1
B200T	1983	BT-24 (BB-1093), BT-25 (BB-1096), BT-26 (BB-1098), BT-27 (BB-1105), BT-29 (BB-1097)	5
B200T	1984	BT-30 (BB-1185)	1
B200T	1987	BT-31 (BB-1264)	1

NOTE: Model 200T - B200T designated "Super King Air". No BT series produced in 1985-1986 calendar years.

Model 300

MODEL	YEAR	CONSTRUCTOR NUMBER	TOTAL DELIVERED
300	1984	FA-1 - FA-27	27
300	1985	FA-28 - FA-87	60
300	1986	FA-88 - FA-111	23
300	1987	FA-112 and after	
300	1987-88	FF-1 - FF-19*	19
300	1987	FA-112 - FA-138	27
300	1988	FA-139 - FA-171	33
300	1989	FA-172 - FA-204	33
300	1990	FA-205 - FA-215	11
300	1991	FA-216 - FA-219	4
300	1992	FA-220	

*NOTE: FF-1 - FF-19 sold to Federal Aviation Administration with deliveries beginning in 1987 through 1988. Model 300 modified for national airway/navigation system surveillance.

NOTE: Model 300 designated "Super King Air".

Model 350 (B300)

MODEL	YEAR	CONSTRUCTOR NUMBER	TOTAL DELIVERED
350	1990	FL-1 - FL-34	34
350	1991	FL-35 - FL-69	35
350	1992	FL-70	

Model 350C Series

MODEL	YEAR	CONSTRUCTOR NUMBER	TOTAL DELIVERED
350C	1990	FM-1	1
350C	1991	FM-2 - FM-3	2
350C	1992	FM-4	

NOTE: Model 350C equipped with cargo door

Model 400

MODEL	YEAR	CONSTRUCTOR NUMBER	TOTAL DELIVERED
400	1986	RJ-3, RJ-9 - RJ-16	8
400	1987	RJ-17 - RJ-34	18
400	1988	RJ-35 - RJ-53 (RJ-51 converted to RK-1)	18
400	1989	RJ-54 - RJ-64	11
400	1990	(not built - production terminated)	
400A	1990	RK-1	1
400A	1991	RK-2 - RK-31	30
400A	1992	RK-32	

NOTE: Model 400 designated "Beechjet".

Model 400T Series - U.S. Air Force T1-A Jayhawk

MODEL	YEAR	CONSTRUCTOR NUMBER	TOTAL DELIVERED
400T	1992	TT-1	

Model 1900 Series

MODEL	YEAR	CONSTRUCTOR NUMBER	TOTAL DELIVERED
1900	1983	UA-2, UA-3	2
1900C	1984	UB-1 - UB-28	28
1900C	1985	UB-29 - UB-50	22
1900C	1986	UB-51 - UB-66	15
1900C	1987	UB-67 and after	
1900C	1987	UB-67 - UB-74	8
1900C	1988	Production terminated	
1900C-1	1987	UC-1 and after*	

*NOTE: Model 1900C-1 c/n UC-1 and after equipped with 670-gallon integral(wet) wing fuel system. All Model 1900 and Model 1900C are designated "1900 Airliner" except executive version designated "King Air Exec-Liner".

MODEL	YEAR	CONSTRUCTOR NUMBER	TOTAL DELIVERED
1900C-1 (C-12J)	1987	UD-1 - UD-6	6

NOTE: UD-1 - UD-6 for U.S. Army National Guard units. Equipped with 670-gallon integral (wet) wing fuel system.

MODEL	YEAR	CONSTRUCTOR NUMBER	TOTAL DELIVERED
1900C-1	1987	UC-1 - UC-17	17
1900C-1	1988	UC-18 - UC-52	35
1900C-1	1989	UC-53 - UC-91	39
1900C-1	1990	UC-92 - UC-138	47
1900C-1	1991	UC-139 - UC-174	36
1900C-1	1992	UC-175	
C-12J	1987	UD-1, UD-2, UD-4, UD-6 (Air National Guard)	4
C-12J	1988	UD-3 & UD-5 (Air National Guard)	2

Model 1900D Series

MODEL	YEAR	CONSTRUCTOR NUMBER	TOTAL DELIVERED
1900D	1991	UE-1 - UE-3	3
1900D	1992	UE-5	

Model 2000/2000A

MODEL	YEAR	CONSTRUCTOR NUMBER	TOTAL DELIVERED
2000	1989	NC-1 - NC-3	3
2000	1990	NC-4 - NC-14	11
2000	1991	NC-15 - NC-20	6
2000A	1991	NC-21 - NC-25	5
2000A	1992	NC-26	

1. Walter Beech leased two buildings of the Cessna Aircraft Company's factory to build the first Beechcraft biplanes. Cessna's Board of Directors approved the lease but Clyde Cessna himself was not involved with the transaction nor the firm that bore his name in April, 1932. Cessna and his son, Eldon, had formed their own airplane company and were building specialized racers in a small facility near the Stearman plant in south Wichita. Later, in 1933, the Cessnas were building famed racing pilot Johnny Livingston's CR-3 in the ex-Travel Air facility before Beech transferred production there during the spring of 1934. Although Ted Wells was responsible for the Model 17R's design, he received valuable assistance from co-engineers Jack Wassal, Cecil Barlow, Wayne Dalrymple, Harry Soderstrom and Willard Bashshaw.

2. Two Model 17R were built, c/n 1 and c/n 2. Both were manufactured in the Cessna factory. Welded steel tube, truss-type spars were used with wood ribs and fabric covering over the wings. Because of persistant cracks and breakage of the streamlined steel brace wires on the empennage, steel tubing was substituted and worked well on c/n 2, NC58Y, as did the full-swiveling tailwheel that greatly improved ground handling characteristics. First 17R, NC499N, also received full-swiveling tailwheel before delivery to Ethyl Corporation.

3. The A17FS was originally built for the MacRobertson Race, to be flown by Robert Fogg and Louise McPhetridge von Thaden. However, it was withdrawn prior to the event and sold to the Civil Aeronautics Authority, who flew the 710 hp A17FS several years before it was reportedly dismantled around 1937.

4. Beechcrafter Virgil Adamson sailed to Japan and assisted the Japanese in assembly of the two C17E biplanes. Beech's first amphibian, the SC17B, handled well on water but poorly on land because the trailing edge of the floats dragged on the ground, making turns very difficult. The project was eventually abandoned but was a worthwhile experiment.

5. The Model G17S was virtually a hand-built flying machine. It took hundreds of man-hours to construct its intricate spruce fairings, weld its steel tube fuselage and fabricate its wooden wings. Labor costs were simply too high after the war to achieve economical production. The basic design of the Staggerwing did not lend itself to adoption of mass production techniques, further discouraging its future. At $29,000, the G17S could not hope to compete with the all-metal, swift and modern Model 35 Bonanza that sold for only $7,975 in 1946.

6. Ted Wells and Walter Beech were aware of the Lockheed Model 12 transport that featured twin tails, but they wanted their airplane to be slightly smaller. Although stories have circulated over the years that Beech simply copied the Lockheed design, there is no evidence to that effect and it seems quite unlikely since men like Wells and Beech needed no inspiration from other designers to be innovative. The most substantial reason for the Model 18 possessing two vertical stabilizers can be traced to the art of stress analysis in the mid-1930s. Ted Wells was thoroughly familiar with analysis of steel tube truss-type structures. He had been working with them for 10 years by 1936, but the all-metal, semi-monocoque structure of the Model 18 presented some unique and difficult problems for stress analysis, particularly because Wells and his tiny staff had virtually no experience with all-metal airframes. A single, conventional vertical stabilizer could have been used on the new Beechcraft, but there was one glitch: the torsional stresses imposed on the aft fuselage under single-engine conditions proved to be a somewhat nebulous phenomenon, not fully understood by many aeronautical engineers of the day. To avoid problems with analyzing such stresses and to ensure a safe design, Wells elected to use two tails...a configuration that would make stress analysis (and therefore certification) an easier task. Mounting the two tails outboard retained the total area needed to maintain directional control on one engine and proved to be the best overall configuration.

7. Exactly how many Model 18 were built from 1937 to 1969 is uncertain. Beech Aircraft Corporation claims 5,680 airplanes were built during World War Two and 1,861 commercial units were produced for a grand total of 7,541. However, other records indicate that 1,914 commercial Model 18 were built from 1946 to 1969. When these are added to the prewar number of 202 airplanes indicated by Beech records, plus war production the grand total is 7,796. Most historians agree that somewhere between 7,000 and 8,000 Model 18 were produced so the 7,796 figure may be reasonably accurate.

8. The Model 34 Twin Quad was not the first airplane to use two engines mounted in the wings driving a single propeller. The German Heinkel He 177 long-range, heavy bomber used a very similar installation during World War Two. Like the Twin Quad, the He 177 featured two engines coupled together driving a single propeller through a reduction gearbox. Engines were Daimler-Benz DB 606A developing 2,700 hp each.

9. The following list gives Beech constructor number for the six USAF L-23E airplanes according to Beech records. Commercial equivalent was Model D50:

L-23E	c/n DH-2	Delivered April, 1956
L-23E	c/n DH-18	Delivered April, 1956
L-23E	c/n DH-79	Delivered May, 1956
L-23E	c/n DH-80	Delivered June, 1956
L-23E	c/n DH-90	Delivered July, 1956
L-23E	c/n DH-91	Delivered July, 1956

10. Certain Model 58TC and Model 58P airplanes were reworked in the field by Beech service engineering teams. Beech Kit #102-5010 was installed that increased gross weight of both models from 6,100 pounds to 6,200 pounds. The kit also provided modifications that changed engine horsepower from 310 to 325 hp, redesignating the powerplants as TSIO-520-LB1C WB1. The modified airplanes were: Model 58TC: c/n TK-85 -c/n TK-91; Model 58P: c/n TJ-169 - c/n TJ-192.

11. The following list contains Beech constructor number and military serial number for the L-23/U-8-series Model 50 Twin Bonanza and U-8F-series Model 65 Queen Air:

YEAR	MODEL	BEECH C/N	MILITARY S/N
1952	L-23B/U-8D	LH-9	52-1801
1956	L-23E/U-8D	DH-88 - DH-91	56-4039, 56-4041, 56-4043, 56-4044
1957	L-23D/U-8D	LH-96 - LH-151	56-3695 - 56-3718 57-3084 - 57-3101 57-6077 - 57-6090
1957	RL-23D/RU-8D	RLH-1 - RLH-8	57-6029 - 57-6036
1958	L-23D/U-8D	LH-152 - LH-180	57-6091 - 57-6094 58-1329 - 58-3059
1958	RL-23D/RU-8D	RLH-9 - RLH-48 RLH-49 - RLH-60	57-6037 - 57-6076 58-3048 - 58-3059
1959	RU-8D	LHC-3 - LHC-10 LH-192 - LH-195	58-1357 - 58-1364 59-2535 - 59-2538
1959	RU-8D	RLH-61 - RLH-93	58-3060 - 58-3092
1959	U-8F	L-3 - L-5	58-1354 - 58-1356
1960	U-8G	LHE-6 - LHE-16	56-3710, 58-3060, 58-3092, 58-1332, 58-3057, 58-3059, 58-3093, 58-3062,

APPENDIX C - FOOTNOTES

			58-1331, 58-3055, 58-1336
1960	U-8F	LF-8 - LF-24	60-3453 - 60-3463
			60-5386 - 60-5390
			66-15365
1961	U-8F	LF-25 - LF-29	61-2426 - 61-2430
1962	U-8F	LF-30 - LF-74	61-3832 - 62-3875
			63-7975
1963	U-8F	LF-75, LF-76	63-13636
			63-13637
1963	NU-8F/YU-21	LG-1 63-12902	

NOTE: LG-1 was first turboprop U-8, with two PT6-6 engines.

12. The following list contains Beech constructor numbers and military serial numbers for the A90-1 - A90-4-series Model 90 King Air and U-21F Model A100 King Air:

1967	A90-1/U-21A	LM-1 - LM-77	66-18000 - 66-18076
		LM-78 - LM-84	67-18078 - 67-18084
		LM-85, LM-86	67-18086, 67-18088
		LM-87 - LM-89	67-18090 - 67-18092
		LM-90 - LM-91	67-18094 - 67-18095
1967	A90-2/RU-21B	LS-1 - LS-3	67-18077, 67-18087
			67-18093
1967	A90-3/RU-21C	LT-1, LT-2	67-18085, 67-18089
1968	A90-1/U-21A	LM-92 - LM-99	67-18096 - 67-18103
		LM-112 - LM-114	67-18116 - 67-18118
1968	A90-1/RU-21A	LM-108 - LM-111	67-18112 - 67-18115
1968	A90-1/RU-21D	LM-100 - LM-107	67-18104 - 67-18111
		LM-115 - LM-117	67-18119 - 67-18121
1969	A90-1/RU-21D	LM-118 - LM-124	67-18122 - 67-18128
1971	A90-1/U-21G	LM-125 - LM-141	70-15891 - 70-15907
1971	A90-4/RU-21E RU-21H	LU-1 - LU-16	70-15875 - 70-15890
1971	U-21F	B-95 - B-99	70-15908 - 70-15912

BIBLIOGRAPHY

ARCHIVAL RECORDS

1. Beech Aircraft Corporation (A Raytheon Company): production records, constructor number files, company archives, marketing and engineering data from 1932 to 1987.

HISTORICAL AND TECHNICAL PUBLICATIONS

1. Ball, Larry A.: Those Incomparable Bonanzas; McCormick-Armstrong Co.; 1971.

2. Christy, Joe; The Complete Guide To Single-Engine Beechcrafts; TAB Books; 1979.

3. McDaniel, William H. and Beech Aircraft Corporation; The History of Beech; McCormick-Armstrong Co.; 1982.

4. Smith, Robert T. and Lempicke, Thomas A.; Staggerwing!; Cody Publications; 1979.

Edward H. Phillips is an avid aero historian and researcher who has a special interest in the aircraft and companies that have made Wichita, Kansas the "Air Capital of the World." His interest in Beechcraft airplanes and their history was strengthened when he came to work for Beech Aircraft Corporation in 1978 after graduating from the University of North Dakota. He is an active general aviation pilot and flight instructor. In addition to BEECHCRAFT – PURSUIT OF PERFECTION, Mr. Phillips has written three other books on Wichita aviation history including TRAVEL AIR – WINGS OVER THE PRAIRIE which traces Walter Beech's rise to fame in the aircraft industry.

AT-7 just off the ground from Hondo Field, Texas with the gear beginning to go up. (Ed Kueppers collection).

88

Interior of AT-7 "Navigator" showing the three student seats and the overhead astrodome through which celestial readings were taken. (Ed Kueppers collection).

Excellent view of the astrodome on an AT-7. All photos in this series were taken by Bernard W. Gouette for the Army Air Force News Service. (Ed Kueppers collection).

Interior view of AT-7 looking forward. Student positions as well as the cockpit are visible. Oxygen bottles and parachute await the students at Hondo, Texas. (Ed Kueppers collection).

INDEX

Back cover: D18's on the line, 1946. Photo by Victor Keppler.

Beechcraft Highlights

1932 – Introduction of first aircraft built by the new Beech Aircraft Company — the Beechcraft Model 17.

1933 – Texaco Trophy race at Miami Air Races. Won by E.H. Wood in No. 1 Beechcraft Model 17.

1936 – First, second and fourth places in Unlimited Race for Frank E. Phillips Trophy at Denver Mile-High Air Races won by Beechcraft Model 17s. First place winner piloted by Bill Ong.

1936 – National speed record for women set by Louise Thaden in a Beechcraft Model 17 at St. Louis, 197.958 mph.

1936 – Bendix Transcontinental Speed Dash and Bendix trophy. Won by Louise Thaden and Blanche Noyes in a Beechcraft Model 17.

1936 – Beechcraft Model 17 carried to Germany aboard dirigible Hindenberg for Capt. James Haizlip to begin flying tour of Europe.

1937 – U.S. women's speed record — 203.895 mph — set by Jacqueline Cochran in a Beechcraft Model D17W.

1937 – Unlimited Race for Frank E. Phillips Trophy. Won by Art Chester in a Beechcraft Model 17.

1937 – Introduction of the Beechcraft Model 18.

1939 – Macfadden Cross-Country Race. Won by Max Constant in a Beechcraft Model D17W.

1939 – New York-to-Miami sports record. Won by Max Constant in a Beechcraft Model D17W.

1939 – Seattle-to-Alaska Air Speed Record. The 1,900 miles were flown in 10 hours, 20 minutes by Kenneth Neese in a Beechcraft Model 17.

1939 – National women's altitude record — 30,052.43 feet — set in a Beechcraft Model 17 by Jacqueline Cochran.

1939 – Skis-mounted Beechcraft Model 17 sets altitude record over South Pole in "Snow Cruiser" expedition of Admiral Byrd and the United States Antarctic Service.

1940 – On-to-Miami race for Macfadden Trophy won in a Beechcraft Model 18. (H.C. Rankin, pilot; Walter H. Beech, co-pilot) 1,084 miles in 4 hours, 37 minutes, at an average speed of 234 mph.

1945 – First flight of Beechcraft Model 35 Bonanza.

1948 – Final delivery of Beechcraft Model 17, to Ohio Oil Company.

1949 – World record for non-stop distance flying for planes of Bonanza category. Capt. Bill Odom in a Beechcraft Bonanza from Honolulu to Oakland, 2,406.9 miles in 22 hours, 6 minutes.

1949 – World record for non-stop distance for all light planes. Capt. Bill Odom in a Beechcraft Bonanza from Honolulu to Teterboro, N.J., 4,957.24 miles in 36 hours, 2 minutes.

1951 –

1952 – Around-the-world flight by Congressman Peter F. Mack, Jr., in the same Beechcraft Bonanza Model 35 flown by Bill Odom. Mack covered 30 countries on his solo flight.

1952 – World speed record for light planes — 225.776 km. per hour (140.29 mph) — set by Paul Burniat of Brussels, Belgium, in a Beechcraft Bonanza.

1953 – Beechcraft Bonanzas finished first, second, third and fourth in first annual Jaycee Transcontinental Air Cruise, Philadelphia to Palm Desert, Calif. W.H. Hinselman won first place and O.A. Beech Trophy.

1953 – Beechcraft D18S, owned by F.C. Castelli Company, won Wings Field Regatto, at Ambler, Pa. and O.A. Beech Trophy.

1953 – Mrs. Marion Hart, 61-year-old sportswoman, flew non-stop from Newfoundland to Ireland in a Beechcraft Bonanza.

1954 – Mrs. Ann Waddell won O.A. Beech Trophy for fastest speed in annual Skylady Derby, Raton, N.M., to Kansas City, Mo., in a Beechcraft Bonanza.

1954 – Three Beechcraft Bonanzas finished first, second and third in the second annual Jaycee Transcontinental Air Cruise from Philadelphia to Palm Desert, Calif. W.C. Butler won first place and O.A. Beech Trophy.

1955 – Mrs. Ann Waddell flew a Beechcraft Bonanza to win the Skylady Derby, Little Rock, Ark., to Raton, N.M.

1956 – Beechcraft enters missile target field with production of Beechcraft KDB-1 for the U.S. Navy.

1956 – Beechcraft Bonanzas win first and second place in the Powder Puff Air Derby — Winning pilot, Frances Bera, in a Beechcraft Bonanza E35.

1957 – Beechcraft Bonanzas win first and third place in the Powder Puff Air Derby — Winning pilot, Alice Roberts, in a Beechcraft Bonanza C35.

1958 – Beechcraft Bonanza wins first place in the Powder Puff Air Derby — Winning pilot, Frances Bera, in a Beechcraft Bonanza A35.

1958 – World record for non-stop distance flying for all light planes. Capt. Pat Boling in a Beechcraft J35 Bonanza from Manila to Pendleton, Ore., 6,856.32 miles, Great Circle distance. (Total miles actually flown — 7,090 in 45 hours, 43 minutes.)

1960 – Beechcraft Model 55 Baron introduced.

1960 – Beechcraft Model 65 Queen Air establishes a new World Altitude Record of 34,862 feet for airplanes in its class — pilot James D. Webber.

1961 – Beechcraft Bonanza wins first place in the Powder Puff Air Derby — Winning pilot, Frances Bera, in a Beechcraft Bonanza E35.

1962 – Beechcraft Bonanza wins first place in the Powder Puff Air Derby — Winning pilot, Mrs. Frances Bera, in a Beechcraft Bonanza F35.

1964 – Turbine-powered, pressurized Beechcraft King Air 90 introduced.

1966 – Beechcraft C55 Baron, piloted by Robert and Joan Wallick, sets round-the-world record for piston-engine aircraft: 23,629 miles; 5 days, 6 hours, 17 minutes.

1967 – Beechcraft Bonanza wins first place in the Powder Puff Air Derby — Winning pilot, Judy Wagner in a Beechcraft Bonanza K35.

1968 – Beechcrafts win first, second and third places in 18th Angel Derby, April 22-25, Managua, Nicaragua, to Panama City, Fla. — Judy Wagner in Beechcraft Bonanza K35. Janis Hobbs in Beechcraft Musketeer and Pat McEwen in Beechcraft Bonanza S35.

1969 – Final delivery of Beechcraft Model 18, to C. Itoh & Co. of Japan, ending the longest continuous production record of any airplane in aviation history.

1969 – Beech Aircraft cryogenic gas storage system supports Apollo XI spacecraft in putting men on the moon for the first time.

1970 – Beechcraft 99A Airliner wins London, England-to-Sydney, Australia Air Race, in 48 hours, 15 minutes, 50 seconds, piloted by Capt. Tom E. Lampitt and crew.

1971 – Beechcraft Bonanza A36 sets record speed-over-a-recognized-course for Class C-1.d Group I aircraft in flying from New York to London, 3,443.56 miles, in 17 hours, 22 minutes, 54 seconds, at average speed of 198.8 mph — piloted by Louise Sacchi.

1971 – Beechcraft Baron B55 sets Speed-Around-the-World record for piston-engine aircraft — 24,800 miles in 5 days, 5 hours, 57 minutes, at elapsed time average speed of 197.77 mph — Travor K. Broughan, pilot, R.N. Dickeson, crewman.

1972 – Beech Aircraft cryogenic gas storage system supports Apollo 17 spacecraft in the sixth and final manned moon landing mission for the NASA Space Exploration Program.

1973 – Beechcraft Super King Air 200 type certificated, December 14, 1973.

1973 – Skylab Spacecraft Missions mark 14th, 15th and 16th space flights for Beech Aircraft's Apollo cryogenic gas storage system.

1975 – Beech wins award of estimated $26 million multi-year contract for new VSTT Army missile target.

1975 – Beechcraft Bonanza A36 wins first place in Powder Puff Derby at average speed of 204.33 mph. Winning pilot, Trina Jarish.

1975 – Beech Aircraft cryogenic gas storage system supports 138-earth-orbit mission of Apollo-Soyuz Test Project.

1975 – Beechcraft Duke sets round-the-world speed record for piston-engine aircraft covering the 24,854 miles in 5 days, 2 hours, 15 minutes, averaging 198.8 mph. Australian pilots Denys Dalton and Terry Gwynn-Jones flew Brisbane-to-Brisbane.

1975 – Beechcraft Model D17S (C-43) joins Beechcraft AT-11 and Beechcraft C45H in exhibit of World War II aircraft at the U.S. Air Force Museum at Wright Field, Dayton, Ohio.

1975 – "Waikiki Beech"/"Friendship Flame" Beechcraft Bonanza 35, which set non-stop distance records in 1949, goes on permanent exhibit in the National Air and Space Museum, Smithsonian Institution, Washington, D.C.

1976 – Beechcraft D18S "Twin Beech" added to classic aircraft on exhibit at the National Air and Space Museum, Smithsonian Institution, Washington, D.C.

1976 – 2,000th B55 Baron is delivered.

1977 – Roll-out of the 10,000th Beechcraft Bonanza Model 35 on February 18, 1977.

1977 – Walter H. Beech, co-founder of Beech Aircraft Corporation, inducted into the Aviation Hall of Fame.

1977 – Beechcraft Bonanza S35 sets new record for the shortest elapsed time around the world in a single-engine, piston aircraft. Jack Rodd and Harold Benham circled the globe in 10 days, 23 hours and 33 minutes.

1977 – Beechcraft Bonanza F33A sets FAI-sanctioned class record for flying 4,300 miles non-stop from New York City to Munich, Germany in 25 hours, 48 minutes — Piloted by Dieter Schmitt of West Germany.

1978 – Beechcraft Bonanza wins All-Women's International Air Race (Angel Derby), from Dallas to Freeport, Bahamas. Pilot, Judy Wagner.

1978 – Beechcraft King Air C90 sets three world records for turboprop business aircraft. Includes record for speed over a recognized course (233.24 mph and 206.21 mph) and distance in a straight line (2,033.91 miles). Pilots F.T. Elliott, Jr. and Thomas Clements flying from San Francisco to Poughkeepsie, N.Y.

1978 – Beechcraft Bonanza wins Republic of South Africa's State President's Trophy Air Race. Piloted by Graeme Conlyn and Nigel Forrester of South Africa.

1978 – Beechcraft Bonanza V35B flies 5,000 miles over the North Pole non-stop Anchorage to Munich. Time enroute 32 hours and 28 minutes. Pilot Dieter Schmitt.

1979 – Beechcraft Bonanza F33A sets world speed record for NAA Clc aircraft between Fresno, Calif., and Las Vegas, Nev. Pilot Marie McMillan.

1979 – Beechcraft Bonanza A36 sets world speed record for this class aircraft from Sacramento, to Los Angeles, Calif. Speed 220 mph. Pilot Jeanette Fowler.

1979 – Salina Division rolls out 500th Duke.

1979 – 100th C-12 delivered to U.S. Army.

1980 – Beechcraft Aircraft & Raytheon Co. complete merger, February 8.

1980 – Beechcraft Sundowner wins Republic of South Africa's State President's Trophy Air Race. Pilots Maureen Forrester and Juliett Serrurier were the first all-women team to win the race.

1980 – Turbocharged Beechcraft Bonanza A36TC flies non-stop New York to Munich in 16 hours, 18 minutes. Pilot Dieter Schmitt.

1980 – Beechcraft Bonanza C33A wins All-Women's International Air Race (Angel Derby), from Corpus Christi, Tex. to Columbia, S.C. Pilots, Pat Jetton and Elinor Johnson.

1980 – Cutaway airframe of Beechcraft Bonanza joins Bonanza 35 in exhibit at the National Air and Space Museum, Smithsonian Institution, Washington, D.C.

1980 – Olive Ann Beech, co-founder and chairman of Beech Aircraft Corporation, accepts aviation's highest honor as the first woman to receive the National Aeronautic Association's coveted Wright Brothers Memorial Trophy.

1981 – Beech cryogenic gas storage system supports first flight of Space Shuttle Orbiter "Columbia".

1981 – Beechcraft Bonanza E33C wins All-Women's International Air Race (Angel Derby), from Los Angeles to Acapulco, Mexico. Pilot, Judy Wagner.

1981 – Olive Ann Beech, co-founder and chairman of Beech Aircraft Corporation, inducted into the Aviation Hall of Fame (Walter H. Beech, her husband and co-founder of Beech Aircraft, was so honored in 1977). With Mrs. Beech's induction, they became the second husband-and-wife team to receive the honor.

1981 – Olive Ann Beech, co-founder and chairman of Beech Aircraft Corporation, receives The Wings Club Distinguished Achievement Award for 1981, at its annual awards program in New York City, for "dedicated pioneering contribution to the design and manufacture of personal and business aircraft leading to the development of the world's foremost general aviation industry."

1982 – 50th Year Anniversary Open House, June 5, 1982.

1983 – Starship unveiled at NBAA October, 1983.

1983 – Beechcraft 1900 Airliner type certified November 22, 1983.

1984 – Beech receives $23.5 million contract for C-12 military airplanes.

1985 – Beech presented Defense Quality Excellence Award by the Defense Logistics Agency of the Department of Defense.

1985 – Beech introduces 530 mph Beechjet.

1986 – First flight of Beechcraft Starship I.

1986 – First Beechjet rolled out.

1986 – Thomas L. Phillips named chairman of the board.

1986 – Beech airplanes provide escort for historic Voyager world flight.

1987 – Max E. Bleck elected president of Beech Aircraft.

1988 – Starship achieves FAA certification.

1988 – Beech delivers first Super King Air 300 flight inspection aircraft to FAA.

1989 – Introduction of the Beech 1900D.

1989 – Introduction of the Super King Air 350.

1989 – Transfer of Beechjet manufacturing from Japan to the United States completed.

1990 – U.S. Air Force selects Beechjet for Tanker-Transport Training System (TTTS) Mission.

1991 – Beech President Max Bleck elected president of Raytheon Company.

1991 – Jack Braly elected president of Beech.

1991 – Beechcraft Bonanza F33A sets FAI-sanctioned class record for flying non-stop from Washington D.C. to Berlin, Germany in 23 hours, 29 minutes — Piloted by Dieter Schmitt of Germany.

1991 – Introduction of the King Air C90B at NBAA.

1992 – First T-1A Jayhawk delivered to U.S. Air Force.

1992 – Beechcraft Bonanza B36TC sets FAI-sanctioned class record for flying from San Francisco to New York in 11 hours, 20 minutes — Piloted by Tim Dolenz and Tony Marlow of Beech Aircraft, and Fred George of FLYING Magazine.

1992 – Delivery of the 50,000th Beechcraft, a King Air C90B, to Charlie Marshall on March 23, 1992.